Message for the Sick and Elderly

Message for the Sick and Elderly

The 25th & 26th Flash from the
Risale-i Nur Flashes Collection

Bediuzzaman Said Nursi

Islamic Book Trust
Kuala Lumpur

Published by
Islamic Book Trust
607 Mutiara Majestic
Jalan Othman
46000 Petaling Jaya
Selangor, Malaysia
www.ibtbooks.com

Islamic Book Trust is affiliated with The Other Press.

Perpustakaan Negara Malaysia   Cataloguing-in-Publication Data

Nursi, Said, 1873-1960
    Message for the Sick and Elderly / Bediuzzaman Said Nursi.
    ISBN 978-967-0526-39-3
    1. Health--Religious aspects--Islam.
    1. Title.
    297.57

Printed by
SS Graphic Printers (M) Sdn Bhd
Lot 7 & 8, Jalan TIB 3, Taman Industri Bolton,
68100 Batu Caves, Selangor Darul Ehsan.

Contents

PART TWO

Treatise for the Elderly

Bediuzzaman Said Nursi
and *Risale-i Nur*

Courtesy: www.bediuzzamansaidnursi.org/

Bediuzzaman Said Nursi was born in 1876 in Eastern Turkey (the Village of Nurs) and died in 1960 in Urfa in Turkey. Readers may refer to his biography for details of his long and exemplary life, which spanned the last decades of the Ottoman Empire, its collapse after the First World War and the setting up of the Republic, then the twenty-five years of Republican Peoples' Party rule, well-known for the measures taken against Islam, followed by the ten years of Democrat rule, when conditions eased a little for Bediuzzaman.

Here we shall mention just a few points which are relevant to the *Risale-i Nur* and will assist in understanding The Words. With this same aim some general points about the *Risale-i Nur* are included, and the method, which is particular to Bediuzzaman, that it employs for teaching the Qur'anic truths.

Bediuzzaman displayed an extraordinary intelligence and ability to learn from an early age, completing the normal course of *Madrasa* (religious school) education at the early age of fourteen, when he obtained his diploma. He became famous for both his prodigious memory and his unbeaten record in debating with other religious scholars. Another characteristic Bediuzzaman displayed from an early age was an instinctive dissatisfaction with the existing education system, which when older he formulated into comprehensive proposals for its reform.

The heart of these proposals was the bringing together and joint teaching of the traditional religious sciences and the modern sciences, together with the founding of a university in the Eastern Provinces of the Empire, the Medresetü'z-Zehra, where this and his other proposals would be put into practice. In 1907 his endeavours in this field took him to Istanbul and an audience with Sultan Abdulhamid. Although subsequently he twice received approval of the funds for the construction of his university, and its foundations were laid in 1913, it was never completed due to war and the vicissitudes of the times.

Contrary to the practice of religious scholars at that time, Bediuzzaman himself studied and mastered almost all the physical and mathematical sciences, and later studied philosophy, for he believed that it was only in this way that Islamic theology (*Kalām*) could be renewed and successfully answer the attacks to which the Qur'an and Islam were then subject.

Bediuzzaman himself described an event in his youth which was decisive in giving him direction. It was learning of the explicit threats to the Qur'an made by Gladstone, the British Secretary for the Colonies. Gladstone's stated intention to discredit the Qur'an, since it was the only way the British could truly dominate the Muslim peoples and achieve their inauspicious ambitions aroused an overpowering reaction in Bediuzzaman.

He vowed: "I shall prove and demonstrate to the world that

the Qur'an is an undying, inextinguishable Sun!" From that time he strove to employ his superior knowledge of both the traditional religious and the modern sciences in the service of the Qur'an; to prove its miraculousness, defend it against the attacks which were largely in the name of science and progress, and relate its truths in the light of modern advances in knowledge. He sought to prove that contrary to the claims of its enemies, the Qur'an was the source of true progress and civilization, and in addition, since this was the case, Islam would dominate the future, despite its relative decline and regression at that time.

In the course of time, the physical sciences had been dropped from *Madrasa* education, which had contributed directly to the Ottoman decline relative to the advance of the West. Now, in the 19th and early 20th centuries, Europe had gained dominance over the Islamic world, and in efforts to extend its dominance, was attacking the Qur'an and Islam in the name of science and progress in particular, falsely claiming them to be incompatible. Within the Empire too were a small minority who favoured adopting Western philosophy and civilization.

Thus, all Bediuzzaman's endeavour was to prove and demonstrate the falseness of these accusations, and that far from being incompatible with science and progress, the Qur'an was the source of true progress and civilization, and in addition, since this was the case, Islam would dominate the future.

The years up to the end of the First World War were the final decades of the Ottoman Empire and were, in the words of Bediuzzaman, the period of the 'Old Said'. He strove to serve the cause of the Empire and Islam through active involvement in social life and the public domain.

In the War, he commanded the militia forces on the

Caucasian Front against the invading Russians, for which he was later awarded a War Medal. To maintain the morale of his men he himself disdained to enter the trenches inspite of the constant shelling, and it was while withstanding the overwhelming assaults of the enemy that he wrote his celebrated Qur'anic commentary, *Signs of Miraculousness*, dictating to a scribe while on horseback. Stating that the Qur'an encompasses the sciences which make known the physical world, the commentary is an original and important work which brings together the religious and modern sciences in the way Bediuzzaman proposed and explains the miraculousness of the order of the verses and words of the Qur'an. Bediuzzaman was taken prisoner in March 1916 and held in Russia for two years before escaping in early 1918, and returning to Istanbul via Warsaw, Berlin, and Vienna.

The defeat of the Ottomans saw the end of the Empire and its dismemberment, and the occupation of Istanbul and parts of Turkey by foreign forces. These bitter years saw also the transformation of the 'Old Said' into the 'New Said', the second main period of Bediuzzaman's life.

Despite the acclaim he received and services he performed as a member of the *Dar-ül-Hikmet-il-Islâmiye*, and combatting the British, Bediuzzaman underwent a profound mental and spiritual change in the process of which he turned his back on the world, and realizing the inadequacy of the 'human' science and philosophy he had studied as a means of reaching the truth, took the revealed Qur'an as his "Sole Guide".

In recognition of his services to the Independence Struggle, Bediuzzaman was invited to Ankara by Mustafa Kemal (Ataturk), but on arrival there, found that at the very time of the victory of the Turks and Islam, Atheistic ideas were being propagated among the Deputies and officials, and many were lax in performing their religious duties. He published various works which successfully countered this.

Remaining some eight months in Ankara, Bediuzzaman understood the way Mustafa Kemal and the new leaders were going to take, and on the one hand that he could not work alongside them, and on the other that they were not to be combatted in the realm of politics. From some *hadith* Sharif, he understood that the terrible persons and committees of the *Akhir-uz-zaman*, namely the Dajjal and his Committee were starting their destructive activities within the Islamic State of Turkey, and also from the same *hadith*, he concluded that those destructive Anti-Islam Forces can be defeated only by the Spiritual Diamond Sword of the Qur'an. And so, when offered various posts and benefits by Mustafa Kemal, he declined them and left Ankara for Van, where he withdrew into a life of worship and contemplation and teaching; he was seeking the best way to proceed.

Within a short time, Bediuzzaman's fears about the new regime began to be realized: the first steps were taken towards secularization and reducing the power of Islam within the State, and even its eradication from Turkish life. In early 1925 there was a rebellion in the east in which Bediuzzaman played no part, but as a consequence of which was sent into exile in western Anatolia along with many hundreds of others.

Thus unjustly began twenty-five years of exile, imprisonment, and unlawful oppression for Bediuzzaman. He was sent to Barla, a tiny village in the mountains of Isparta Province. However, the attempt to entirely isolate and silence him had the reverse effect, for Bediuzzaman was both prepared and uniquely qualified to face the new challenge:

These years (1926-1934) saw the writing of the *Risale-i Nur*, which silently spread and took root, combatting in the most constructive way the attempt to uproot Islam, and the unbelief and Materialist philosophy it was hoped to instill in the Muslim people of Turkey.

Thus, it may be seen from this that the *Risale-i Nur* was written to expound and explain the truths of the Qur'an and belief to modern man, bewildered as he is by the assaults of materialist philosophy, so that he may attain true and certain belief which will not be shaken by those assaults. In explaining these truths, the *Risale-i Nur* demonstrates the Qur'an's superiority in every respect, and, although "in order not to cause aversion" philosophy's ideas are rarely openly stated, is a refutation of materialist Western philosophy.

It should be stated here that Bediuzzaman was not anti-Western as such,—indeed, he differentiated between harmful and beneficial philosophy, and hoped for the salvation of all mankind—but was uncompromising against the unbelief and atheism which is opposed to religion; in recent times the weapon of this has mostly been materialist philosophies such as Positivism and Naturalism, which use science to justify their ideas.

As the New Said, Bediuzzaman had immersed himself in the Qur'an, searching for a way to relate its truths to modern man. In Barla in his isolation, he began to write treatises explaining and proving these truths, for now the Qur'an itself and its truths were under direct attack. The first of these was on the Resurrection of the Dead, which in a unique style, proves bodily Resurrection rationally, where even the greatest scholars previously had confessed their impotence. He described the method employed in this as consisting of three stages: first God's existence is proved, and His Names and attributes, then the Resurrection of the Dead is "constructed" on these and proved. Bediuzzaman did not ascribe these writings to himself, but said they proceeded from the Qur'an itself, were "Rays shining out of from the truths of Qur'an."

Thus, rather than being a Qur'anic commentary which expounds all its verses giving the immediate reasons for their revelation and the apparent meanings of the words and sentences, the *Risale-i Nur* is what is known as a *Tafseer-i Manawi*, or commentary which expounds the truths of the Qur'an, that is, explains and proves the verses containing the Qur'anic teachings. For there are various sorts of commentaries. The verses mostly expounded in the *Risale-i Nur* are those concerned with the truths of belief, such as the Divine Names and attributes and the Divine activity in the universe, the Divine existence and Unity, Resurrection, Prophethood, Divine Determining or Destiny, and Man's duties of Worship.

Bediuzzaman explains how the Qur'an addresses all men in every age in accordance with the degree of their understanding and development; it has a face that looks to each age. The *Risale-i Nur*, then, explains that face of the Qur'an which looks to this age. We shall now look at further aspects of the *Risale-i Nur* related to this point.

In numerous of its verses, the Holy Qur'an invites man to observe the universe and reflect on the Divine activity within it; following just this method, Bediuzzaman provides proofs and explanations for the truths of belief. He likens the universe to a book, and looking at it in the way shown by the Qur'an, that is, 'reading' it for its meaning, learns of the Divine Names and attributes and other truths of belief. The book's purpose is to describe its Author and Maker; beings become evidences and signs to their Creator. Thus, an important element in the way of the *Risale-i Nur* is reflection or contemplation (*tefekkür*), 'reading' the Book of the Universe in order to increase in knowledge of God and to obtain 'certain' belief in all the truths of belief.

Bediuzzaman demonstrates that the irrefutable truths, such as Divine Unity, arrived at in this way are the only rational and logical explanation of the universe, and making comparisons with Naturalist and Materialist philosophy—which have used science's findings about the universe to deny those truths, show the concepts on which they are based, such as causality and Nature, to be irrational and logically absurd.

Indeed, far from contradicting them, in uncovering the order and working of the universe, science broadens and deepens knowledge of the truths of belief. In the *Risale-i Nur* many descriptions of the Divine activity in the universe are looked at through the eyes of science, and reflect Bediuzzaman's knowledge of it. The *Risale-i Nur* shows that there is no contradiction or conflict between religion and science.

In addition, all these matters discussed in the *Risale-i Nur* are set out as reasoned arguments and proved according to logic. All the most important of the truths of belief are proved so clearly that even unbelievers can see their necessity. And so too, inspired by the Qur'an, even the most profound and inaccessible truths are made accessible by means of comparisons, which bring them close to the understanding like telescopes, so that they are readily understandable by ordinary people and those with no previous knowledge of these questions.

Another aspect of the *Risale-i Nur* related to the face of the

Qur'an which looks to this age, is that it explains everything from the point of view of wisdom; that is, as is mentioned again below, it explains the purpose of everything. It considers things from the point of view of the Divine Name of All-Wise.

Also, following this method, in the *Risale-i Nur* Bediuzzaman solved many mysteries of religion, such as bodily resurrection and Divine Determining and man's will, and the riddle of the constant activity in the universe and the motion of particles, before which man relying on his own intellect and philosophy had been impotent.

While in Barla, Bediuzzaman put the treatise on Resurrection and the pieces that followed it together in the form of a collection and gave it the name of The Words (*Sözler*). The pieces were thirty-two in number, the thirty-third was added later. The treatise on Resurrection became the Tenth Word. The first nine are short, simple pieces describing through the use of comparisons the virtues and benefits of belief and of worship—in the *Risale-i Nur* are many analyses and comparisons of guidance and misguidance, belief and unbelief, which point out the grievous pains of unbelief and demonstrate that man's true happiness and progress are only to be found in recognition of the world's Owner and submission to Him.

The Words that follow the Tenth comprise numerous subjects, all of great importance; among them are the Twelfth and Thirteenth Words and their comparisons between the Qur'an and philosophy; the explanations of Divine Unity, Oneness, and God's closeness to us and our distance from Him in the Sixteenth and Thirty-Second Words; the proofs of the Qur'an's miraculousness in the Twenty-Fifth Word, which answers in particular criticisms made by atheists and scientists; the Twenty-Sixth on Divine

Determining and man's faculty of will; the immortality of man's spirit, the angels and resurrection in the Twenty-Ninth Word; and the nature of man's ego and the transformation of minute particles of the Thirtieth.

The Words was followed by *Mektûbat*, Letters, a collection of thirty-three letters of varying lengths from Bediuzzaman to his students. And this was followed by *Lem'alar*, The Flashes, and *Shualar*, The Rays, which was completed in 1949, included in these last two are Bediuzzaman's defence speeches from the trials at Eskisehir in 1935, and Afyon in 1948-1949. Together with these are the three collections of Additional Letters, for each of Bediuzzaman's main places of exile, *Barla Lahikasi*, *Kastamonu Lahikasi*, and *Emirdag Lahikasi*.

The way the *Risale-i Nur* was written and disseminated was unique, like the work itself. Bediuzzaman would dictate at speed to a scribe, who would write down the piece in question with equal speed; the actual writing was very quick. Bediuzzaman had no books for reference and the writing of religious works was of course forbidden. They were all written therefore in the mountains and out in the countryside. Handwritten copies were then made, these were secretly copied out in the houses of the *Risale-i Nur* 'Students', as they were called, and passed from village to village, and then from town to town, till they spread throughout Turkey. Only in 1946 were *Risale-i Nur* Students able to obtain duplicating machines, while it was not till 1956 that *The Words* and other collections were printed on modern presses in the new, Latin, script. The figure given for hand-written copies is 600,000.

It may be seen from the above figure how the *Risale-i Nur* movement spread within Turkey, despite all efforts to stop it.

After 1950, the period of what Bediuzzaman called 'the Third Said', there was a great increase in the number of Students, particularly among the young and those who had been through the secular education system of the Republic. At the same time the number of Students outside Turkey increased. It is no exaggeration to say that with its conveying the Qur'anic message in a way that addresses and answers modern man's needs, the *Risale-i Nur* played a major role in keeping alive the Islamic faith in Turkey in those dark days, and in the resurgence of Islam that has occurred subsequently.

Above all, the people of this age want reasonable answers to everything, they want to know "why?" And although science has opened up the universe from the minutest sub-atomic particles to the obscurest, most distant reaches of space, it has remained impotent before this question; it has been unable to provide the answer to the question "why?" Whereas, taking its inspiration from the Divine Revelation of the Qur'an, the *Risale-i Nur* looks at things from the point of view of wisdom; it explains the wisdom, purposes and aims of all the various matters it discusses. It points out the purposes of everything, from the universe and all the beings in it and all the realms of creation to man and his comprehensive disposition and his duties of worship; it answers the question "why?"

And in addition provides reasonable, satisfying answers to all sorts of questions to do with belief, life, man, and existence; parts of it are even written in the form of question and answer. One of the *Risale-i Nur's* most important characteristics is this, which accounts for its unparalleled success in saving and strengthening the belief of many hundreds of thousands, and probably millions, of people throughout the world.

Philosophy, and science when in the service of philosophy, cast the world into ultimate meaninglessness and man into a mire of doubts, fears, and ultimate hopelessness. In explaining the Qur'anic message for man in this modern age, the *Risale-i Nur* raises man out that dark hopelessness by illuminating with meaning both himself and the world in which he finds himself.

PART ONE

Message for the Sick

Being the **25th** Flash from the Flashes Collection of *Risale-i Nur*. Volume 3

This treatise was written as a medicine, a solace, a spiritual prescription, and as a visit wishing recovery for those who are ill.

A reminder and an apology

This spiritual prescription, which was written at great speed, has not been revised and has been left as it occurred to my heart. Therefore, I request the readers, and particularly the unwell, not to feel offended by any disagreeable expressions that may be contained within. I also request them to pray for me.

In the Name of God, the Merciful, the Compassionate.

Those who, when a disaster befalls them, say, "Surely we belong to God (as His creatures and servants), and surely to Him we are bound to return."

—Al-Baqarah, 2:156

"And He it is Who gives me food and drink; And Who, when I fall ill, heals me."

—Al-Shu'arā', 26:79-80

In this *Flash*, we explain the twenty-five remedies which may offer true consolation for those who are ill or struck by misfortune, who make up one tenth of humankind.

✺ First Remedy

You who are unhappy in your sickness! Do not be anxious, persevere instead. Your illness is not a loss for you, but a gain, a sort of cure. For life departs like capital. If it yields no fruits, it is wasted. And if it passes in ease and heedlessness, it is short, bringing almost no profit. Illness makes that capital of yours yield huge profits. Moreover, it prevents your life from being short; it holds it back, lengthening or expanding it, so that it may depart after yielding its fruits. Indicating the fact that life lengthens through illness, this proverb is much renowned and widely circulated:

> "The time of disaster is very long;
> the time of enjoyment, very short."

❖ Second Remedy

You who are ill and lacking in perseverance! Do indeed persevere and offer thanks. Your illness may transform each of the minutes of your life that pass in illness into one hour's worship. For worship is of two sorts. One is that which is performed, the other is the sort which is not actually performed, but is suffered and thus leads to sincere supplication. Illnesses and disasters are examples of this sort. By means of these, those afflicted deeply feel their innate impotence and weakness; they take refuge in their All-Compassionate Creator and entreat, thus being able to perform sincere worship. There are authenticated narrations from God's noble Messenger, upon him be peace and blessings, that the times of believers which pass in illness are counted as worship, provided they do not complain about God.[1] It is also reliably narrated from the Messenger and there are reports from saints of spiritual discovery that one minute's illness of some patients who show perseverance with thankfulness equals one hour's worship, and a minute's illness of certain spiritually perfected individuals, equals the worship of a day. Therefore, rather than complaining, be thankful for the illness, which makes one minute of your life the equivalent of a thousand minutes and gains for you a long life.

❖ Third Remedy

You who are impatient in your illness! The fact that all those who come to this world inevitably depart, that the young grow old, and that the world is perpetually turning amidst death and separation, testifies that humankind has not come to this world for enjoyment or pleasure. In addition, although

---

[1] *al-Bukhari,* "Jihad" 134; Ahmad ibn Hanbal, *al-Musnad,* 4:410. (Tr.)

humankind is the most perfect of living beings, the richest of beings in the equipment of life, and can virtually be regarded as their king, because of dwelling on past pleasures and worrying about future troubles, human beings lead a grievous, troublesome life, much lower than the animals. This shows that humankind has not come to this world to live in ease and pleasure. Rather, possessing vast capital, it has come here to work for an eternal life by doing the required trade. The capital given to it is its lifetime.

Were it not for illness, good health and ease would cause heedlessness, presenting the world as pleasant and making people oblivious of the Hereafter. By distracting them from the thought of death and the grave, good health and ease cause them to waste the capital of life on trifles. But illness suddenly gives them awareness, and says to the body:

> "You are not immortal, and have not been left to your own devices. You have a duty. Give up haughtiness; think of the One Who has created you; know that you will enter the grave, and make the necessary preparation!"

Thus, from this perspective, illness is an advisor that never deceives; and it is an admonishing guide. For this reason, rather than complaining about illness, we should be thankful for it. If it gives much trouble and pain, we should show patience.

❊ Fourth Remedy

You who are ill and complaining! It is better for you not to complain, but to give thanks and show patience. For your body, with all its members and your faculties, is not your property. You have not made them, nor have you bought any of your bodily components from any workshop. They are the property of someone else. Their Owner has disposal over His property as He wills.

As stated in The Twenty-Sixth Word (included in *The Words*), a very rich and infinitely skilled clothes designer uses an ordinary man as a model to display his works of art and invaluable wealth in return for wages. For a brief hour, he clothes the model in a jeweled and artistically fashioned garment that he has made. He continues to modify the garment while the model wears it. In order to display his wonderful varieties of art, he cuts the garment, alters it, lengthening it here and shortening it there. Does the model employed for a wage have any right to say, "Your orders to bow and stand up are causing me trouble. Your cutting and shortening of this garment, which must make me more beautiful, spoils my beauty." Can the model accuse the designer of treating him unkindly and unfairly?

You who are ill! As in that simile, the All-Majestic Maker—in order to display the embroideries of His All-Beautiful Names and indeed make you more and more "beautiful"—causes you to undergo numerous, different states and situations in the garment of your body in which He has clothed you, bejeweled as it is with luminous faculties like seeing, hearing, reasoning, and feeling. Just as, through hunger, you learn of His Name, The All-Providing, so too through your illness, you come to know His Name, The All-Healing. Since suffering and disasters manifest the decrees and operations of some of His Names, there are in them gleams of wisdom, and rays of mercy, within which are numerous beauties. If the veil between us and His decrees and acts were to be lifted, you would find many agreeable and beautiful meanings behind the veil of illness, which you are frightened of and dislike.

❖ Fifth Remedy

*Y*ou who are afflicted with illness! I have become convinced through experience at this time that illness is a Divine favor for some people, a gift of mercy. Although I am not worthy of it, for these last eight or nine years, a number of young people have visited me to pray for them because of their illnesses. I have noticed that compared to those of the same age, any unwell young person I have met has begun to think of the Hereafter. They are no longer in the typical intoxication of youth, and have saved themselves to a degree from the animal desires that are embedded in heedlessness. Based on this observation, I would remind them that their bearable illnesses are a Divine favor. I would say,

> "Brother, I am not opposed to this illness of yours. I do not feel compassion for you due to your illness, so that I should pray for you. Try to show good patience until illness awakens you completely, and after it has completed its duty, God willing, the All-Compassionate Creator will cure you."

I would also say to them as follows:

> Because of the calamity of good health, some of your equals in age become heedless, and do not perform the five daily Prayers; they do not think of the grave, forget God, and damage, even destroy, the eternal life for the sake of the superficial pleasure of an hour's worldly life. But with the eye of illness, you see your grave, which you will in any case enter, and the mansions of the Hereafter beyond it, and act accordingly. This means that illness is good health for you,

> while the good health of some of your peers is in fact an illness for them.

✸ Sixth Remedy

You who are sick and complain of your suffering, I say to you: Think of your past life and remember the pleasurable, happy days and the distressing, troubled times. For sure, you will either say, "Oh!" or, "Ah!" That is, your heart and tongue will either say, "All praise and thanks be to God!" or, "Alas, alas!"

Notice that what makes you utter a sigh of relief and say, "All praise and thanks be to God!" is that your thinking of the sufferings and calamities that befell you in the past stirs up a kind of spiritual pleasure and causes your heart to be thankful. For the disappearance of suffering is a pleasure. The passing of sufferings and calamities left a lasting pleasure in the spirit. When it is stirred up through thinking, a pleasure pours forth from the spirit with thanks.

What makes you exclaim, "Alas, alas!" is the pleasurable and happy times you enjoyed in the past. Through cessation, they have left an unending pain in your spirit so that whenever you think of them, that pain is aroused and causes sorrow and regret to pour forth.

Since one day's illicit pleasure sometimes causes a year's spiritual suffering, while the pain of one day's temporary illness brings the pleasure of many days' rewards together with the pleasure of its cessation, think of the result of this temporary illness you are suffering now and the rewards it potentially bears. Say, "This too will pass, God willing!" and, instead of complaining, offer thanks.

Another sixth remedy

You, brother or sister in faith, who think of the pleasures of this world and are distressed by illness! If this world were eternal, and if on our way to eternity there were no death, and if the winds of separation and death did not blow, and if there were no "winters" of the spirit in the calamitous and stormy future, I would have pitied you along with you. But since the world will one day say to us, "Now, it is the time of departure!" and close its ears to our cries, warned by these illness, we must give up our love of it before it drives us out. Before it abandons us, we must try to abandon it in our hearts.

Illness reminds us of this reality and says,

> "Your body is not composed of stone and iron; rather it has been composed of various materials that are subject to partition and dissolution. Give up conceit, be aware of your innate impotence, recognize your Master, know your duties, and learn why you came to the world!"

Illness says this secretly in the ear of the heart.

Also, since the pleasure and enjoyment of this world do not last and, particularly if they are licit, this is distressing and painful, do not weep over their disappearance because of illness. On the contrary, think of the worship you are performing by enduring the illness and the rewards that pertain to the Hereafter, and try to be content.

✸ Seventh Remedy

You who are ill and have lost the pleasures of health! Your illness does not ruin the contentment of the Divine blessing in health; rather, it causes you to taste it more deeply, and increases it. For if something continues uninterruptedly, it loses its effect. The people of truth agree that "things are known through their opposites." For example, were it not for darkness, light would not be known and it would give no pleasure. Without cold, heat would not be recognized, and would remain unpleasant. If there were no hunger, food would offer no delight. If there were no thirst, drinking water would give no satisfaction. Without illness, health and appetite would be without pleasure.

By endowing humans with numerous senses, organs, and faculties that they may taste and recognize the uncountable varieties of His bounties in the universe, the All-Wise Originator shows that He wills that humans may experience all the varieties of His bounties and give continual thanks. Therefore, as He grants good health and appetite, He will certainly give illnesses and pains. I ask you: If you were not suffering this discomfort in your head or hands or stomach, would you be mindful of the pleasure of the Divine favor of the good health in your head or hands or stomach, and offer thanks? Certainly, not only would you not have offered thanks, you would not have even considered it! You would have expended that good health unconsciously and heedlessly, and perhaps even wantonly.

❋ Eighth Remedy

*Y*ou who are sick and now reflecting on the Hereafter! Like soap, sickness washes away the dirt of sins and cleanses. It is established in an authenticated *hadith* that illnesses are expiation for sins. It says,

> "As ripe fruits fall from the tree when it is shaken,
> so the sins of a believer fall away
> with the shaking during illness."[2]

---

[2] *al-Bukhari*, "Marda'" 1, 2, 13; *Muslim*, "Birr" 14. (Tr.)

Sins are perpetual illnesses in the eternal life. They are also illnesses for the heart, conscience, and spirit in this worldly life. If you persevere and do not complain, you are being saved from numerous perpetual illnesses through that temporary illness. But if you do not worry about sins, or are not aware of the afterlife, or do not recognize God, you have such an illness that it is a million times worse than your present illness. Cry out at it, for your heart, spirit, and soul have relations with all the beings in the world. Your connections with them are continually severed through decay, death, and separation, causing innumerable wounds to open up in you. Particularly since you are not aware of the Hereafter and imagine death to be eternal extinction, it is as if you had a body afflicted with uncountable wounds and illnesses. Therefore, what you must do first is to search for belief as the cure for these innumerable spiritual wounds and illnesses of the ailing body. You must correct your creed, and the shortest, most direct way to such a cure is to recognize the Power and Mercy of an All-Powerful One of Majesty through the window of your innate impotence and weakness, which your physical illness shows you beneath the veil of heedlessness that it has rent.

Indeed, one who does not recognize God is afflicted with a worldful of tribulations, while the world of one who recognizes God is full of light and spiritual joy. Everyone is aware of this according to the strength of their belief. The pain of physical illnesses melts away under the spiritual joy, healing, and pleasure that come from belief.

❋ Ninth Remedy

*Y*ou who are ill and acknowledge your Creator! People fear and are distressed by illness because it sometimes leads to death. Since death is frightening to the superficial, heedless view, illnesses that may lead to it cause fear and worry.

So, first of all, know and believe with certainty that the appointed hour of death is certain and does not change. It has many times occurred that the healthy ones weeping beside the seriously ill have died, while the seriously ill have been cured and continue to live.

Secondly, death is not frightening; it is not as it appears to be. Based on the light provided by the wise Qur'an, we have convincingly explained in many parts of the *Risale-i Nur* that for people of belief, death is a discharge from the hardship of the duties of this life. It is also a respite from worship, which is a drill and training in the arena of trials in this world. Moreover, it is a means of reunion with ninety-nine relatives and beloved ones who have already emigrated to the other world. It is also a means of entering the true homeland and eternal abode of happiness. In addition, it is an invitation from the prison of the world to the spacious gardens of Paradise. And it is the time when one receives a wage from the grace of the All-Compassionate Creator in return for a service. Since this is the reality of death, we should view death not as something terrifying, but as the prelude to mercy and happiness.

Moreover, for some of the people of God, the fear of death is not terror of death itself, but rather on account of their hope, through the continuation of the duties of life, that they will gain more merit by performing more good works.

For the people of belief, death is the door to Divine mercy, while for the people of misguidance it is the pit of eternal darkness.

❖ Tenth Remedy

*Y*ou who are ill and worrying needlessly! Your worry is because of the severity of your illness, but your worries make your illness more severe. If you want your illness to be less severe, try not to worry about it. That is, think about the benefits of your illness, the spiritual rewards it brings, and that it will pass quickly. Give up worrying, and cut off the illness at the root.

Indeed, worry doubles the burden of illness; in addition to your physical illness, it causes an immaterial illness in your heart, upon which the physical illness depends and through which it persists. If that worry vanishes through submission, resignation, and thinking of the wisdom inherent in the illness, one of the important roots of the illness will be severed. It becomes less severe and in part disappears. Sometimes a minor physical illness becomes tenfold just through worries and apprehension. When worries and apprehension cease, nine tenths of the illness disappears. In addition to increasing an illness, since worry is an accusation against Divine wisdom, a criticism of Divine Mercy, and a complaint about the All-Compassionate Creator, it causes counter-suffering, and increases illness.

Indeed, just as thankfulness increases favor, so too do complaints increase illnesses and suffering. Furthermore, worry is itself an illness. The cure for it is knowing the wisdom inherent in illness. Since you are now aware of the wisdom in illness and its benefits, apply that ointment to the worry and be relieved. Say,

"Oh!" instead of, "Ah!" and "All praise be to God for every state!" instead of, "Alas!" and "Oh dear!"

✸ Eleventh Remedy

You, brother or sister in faith! You who are sick and impatient! Although your present illness causes you some suffering, all your former illnesses have produced an immaterial contentment for your spirit resulting in your recovery from them, and a spiritual pleasure arising from the reward received for enduring them. There may be no more illnesses from today on, even from this hour, so no pain can come from something that does not exist. And if there is no pain, there is no grief. But since you imagine otherwise, you are showing impatience. For all the times of illness before today have disappeared together with the pains they have caused, leaving the rewards the illness has brought and the pleasure their departure gives. So, when they should give you the feeling of profit and happiness, it is crazy to think of them and feel grieved, or to be impatient. The future days have not come yet. Thinking of them now and feeling grieved and showing impatience with thoughts about a day that does not exist, or an illness that does not exist, or a suffering that does not exist, and thus giving the color of existence to three degrees of non-existence—if that is not crazy, what is?

Since the times of illness before now have given happiness, and since the times subsequent to it and the illnesses and sufferings (you imagine they may bring) are non-existent, do not scatter the power of the patience God Almighty has given you to the right and left, but mobilize it against the pain of the present hour. Say, "O All-Patient One!" and endure it.

✸ Twelfth Remedy

You who on account of illness cannot perform your regular worship or invocations, and regret this! Know that it is stated in a *hadith*,

> "A pious, God revering believer who, due to illness, cannot do the invocations he does normally and regularly, receives an equal reward."[3]

Illness substitutes for the supererogatory Prayers of the ill person who does their obligatory worship as much as possible and shows patience in submissive reliance on God.

Furthermore, illness reminds people of their innate impotence and weakness, and causes them to pray both verbally and through the tongue of their state. God Almighty has created human beings with boundless impotence and weakness so that they continually seek refuge in the Divine Court and pray and supplicate. Since, according to the verse,

> *Say: "My Lord would not care for you were it not for your prayer,"*

> —Al-Furqān, 25:77

the wisdom in the creation of humanity and the reason for its value are sincere prayer, and as illness leads people to such prayers, rather than complaining about illness, we should thank God, and should not turn off the fountain of prayer that has been caused to flow by illnesses.

✸ Thirteenth Remedy

You who are unhappy and complain of your illness! Illness is an important treasure and a very valuable Divine gift for

---

[3] *Abu Dawud, "Jana'iz" 1; Ahmad ibn Hanbal, al-Musnad, 4:418.*

some people. Every ill person can consider their illness from this perspective.

Our appointed hour of death is unknown to us. So, in order to save people from absolute despair and heedlessness and to keep them between fear and hope and in a position from which they may lose neither in the world nor in the Hereafter, God Almighty has concealed the appointed hour of death. Since death can come at any time, if it captures the human being in heedlessness, it may cause great harm to their eternal life. But illness dispels heedlessness, makes people think of their afterlife and reminds them of death and thus prepares them for the Hereafter. They sometimes make such great profit that in twenty days they can gain a rank that they could not otherwise have gained in twenty years.

For instance, from among my friends there were two youths, may God have mercy on them, Sabri from the village of Ilema, and Vezirzade Mustafa from Islamköy. I used to note with amazement that although these two were illiterate and could not serve by copying the *Risale-i Nur*, they were among the foremost in sincerity and the service of belief. I did not know why that was so. After their deaths I understood that both had suffered from a serious illness. Guided by that illness, unlike other heedless youths who did not carry out the obligatory worship, they had great reverence for God, and performed the most valuable services, attaining a state beneficial to the Hereafter. God willing, the trouble of two years' illness was the means to the bliss of millions of years of eternal life. I now understand that the prayers I sometimes offered for their health were maledictions in respect to this world. I hope that my prayers were accepted for their well-being in the Hereafter.

Thus, it is my belief that these two gained a profit equal to that which can be gained through ten years' piety and righteousness (*taqwa*). If, like some young people, they had trusted in their youth and good health and let themselves fall into heedlessness and dissipation, and if death, which is always on the watch, had grasped them right in the midst of the filth of their sins, their graves would have been the lairs of scorpions and snakes, instead of that treasury of lights.

Since there are such benefits in illness, we should not complain about it, but bear it with patient reliance on God, indeed, with gratitude to Him and confidence in His Mercy.

✸ Fourteenth Remedy

You who are sick in that your eyes are afflicted with cataracts! If you knew what a light and spiritual seeing there is beneath the cataracts that may cover a believer's eyes, you would exclaim, "A hundred thousand thanks to my All-Compassionate Lord." I will relate an incident to you to explain this ointment. It is as follows:

One time, the aunt of Süleyman from Barla, who served me for eight years with perfect loyalty and without causing any resentment, became blind. Thinking well of me a hundred times more than was my due, that righteous woman caught me by the door of the mosque and asked me to pray for the recovery of her eyes. I therefore made that blessed woman's righteousness the intercessor for my prayer, and entreated, "O Lord! Restore her sight due to her righteousness." Two days later, an eye specialist from Burdur came and removed the cataracts. But forty days later she again lost her sight. I was much grieved and prayed for her earnestly. I hope that the prayer was accepted for her afterlife, or else my prayer was the most mistaken malediction for her. For there remained only another forty days until her death; forty days later she died—May God have mercy on her.

Thus, rather than looking sorrowfully at the pathetic gardens of Barla with the eye of old age, she profited by being able to gaze on the gardens of Paradise from her grave for forty thousand days, for she had a firm belief and was earnestly righteous.

If a believer loses their sight and enters the grave blind, they may, in accordance with their degree, gaze on the world of light to a much greater extent than the other people of the grave. Just as in this world we see many things that blind believers do not see, if they go from this world with belief, they see to a greater extent than the other people of the grave. As if looking through the most powerful telescopes, they can, in accordance with their degree, see and gaze on the gardens of Paradise as on a movie screen.

Thus, through thanks and patience you can find under the veil that exists on your present eye an eye that is light-filled and light-diffusing and with which you can see and gaze on Paradise above the heavens while under the soil. The eye specialist which will remove the veil from your present eye and enable you to look with that eye is the wise Qur'an.

✸ Fifteenth Remedy

You who are sick and sighing and lamenting! Do not consider the outward aspect of illness and sigh; consider its meaning and be content. If the meaning of illness was not good, the All-Compassionate Creator would not have given illness to His most-beloved servants. A *hadith* says,

> "Those afflicted with the severest trials are the Prophets, then those resembling them, and then those resembling the latter."[4]

That is, those most afflicted with suffering and hardship are the best of people, the most perfect of them. The Prophets, including in particular the Prophet Job, upon him be peace, then the saints, and then those foremost in righteousness after the Prophets and saints have regarded the illnesses they have suffered as sincere worship and gifts from the All-Merciful. They have offered thanks in patience. They have seen these illnesses as surgical operations performed by the compassion of the All-Compassionate Creator.

O you who cry out and lament! If you want to join this light-diffusing caravan, offer thanks in patience. For if you complain, they will not admit you among them. You will fall into the pits of the people of misguidance, and go along a dark road.

Indeed, there are some illnesses which, if they lead to death, are like a sort of martyrdom. They cause one to gain some certain degree of sainthood. For example, like the believing women who die during or because of childbirth,[5] those who die from pains in the abdomen, and by drowning, burning, or the plague, are considered as martyrs.[6] There are also other such blessed illnesses which help to gain a degree of sainthood for those who die from them. Furthermore, since illness lessens the love of the world and attachment to it, it lightens the pain of parting from the world, which is extremely grievous for worldly people. Sometimes it makes such a departure desirable.

---

[4] *at-Tirmidhi*, "Zuhd" 57; *Ibn Majah*, "Fitan" 23. (Tr.)

[5] A child-bearing woman may gain some sort of martyrdom if she dies within forty days after giving birth.

[6] *al-Bukhari*, "Jihad" 30; *Muslim*, "'Imara" 164. (Tr.)

✸ Sixteenth Remedy

*Y*ou who are sick and complain of your distress! Illness induces respect and compassion, which are most important and good for human social life. This saves people from conceited feelings of self-sufficiency, which drives them to unfriendliness and unkindness. For according to the reality stated in,

> *"No indeed, but the human is unruly and rebels, in that he sees himself as self-sufficient".*

—Al-'Alaq, 96: 6–7

a carnal, evil-commanding soul which feels self-sufficient due to good health and well-being does not regard the many causes which are deserving of brotherhood. And they do not feel compassion towards the misfortune-stricken or ill, who should be shown kindness and pity. Yet, whenever they become ill, they are aware of their own innate impotence and neediness, and feel respect towards their sisters and brothers who are worthy of it. They pay respect to their believing brothers and sisters who visit or help them. And they feel human kindness, which originates in fellow-feeling and compassion for the disaster-stricken—a most important Islamic characteristic. Comparing others to themselves, they empathize with them, feel affection for them, and do whatever they can to help them. At the very least they pray for others and pay them a visit of consolation, which is a *Sunnah* act according to the Shari'ah,[7] thus earning reward.

---

[7] *Muslim*, "Birr" 40; *Abu Dawud*, "Jana'iz" 7; *at-Tirmidhi*, "Jana'iz" 2. (Tr.)

✸ Seventeenth Remedy

*Y*ou who are sick and complain of not being able to do good works due to illness! Offer thanks! It is illness that opens to you the door of the most sincere of good works. Illness is a most important means of continuously gaining reward for the sick person and for those who are looking after them for the sake of God; it is, in addition, a means for supplications to be accepted.

Certainly, there is significant reward for believers who look after the sick. Asking after the health of those who are ill and visiting them—provided it does not tax them—is a *Sunnah* act, an act highly recommended by our Prophet, upon him be peace and blessings.[8] It is also expiation for sins. There is a *hadith* which says,

> "Receive the prayers of the ill,
> for their prayers are acceptable."[9]

Especially if the person who is ill is a relative, in particular parents, looking after them is an important form of worship which yields significant rewards. To please an invalid's heart and to console them is like giving alms. Fortunate is the one who pleases the easily-touched hearts of their father and mother when they are ill, and receives their prayer. Indeed, even the angels applaud saying,

> "How good, how blessed that is!
> May God reward them abundantly!"

before faithful scenes of those good offspring who respond to the

---

[8] *al-Bukhari*, "Marda'" 4, 5; *Muslim*, "Salam" 47.
[9] *Ibn Majah* "Jana'iz" 1; al-Bayhaqi, *Shu'ab al-Iman*, 6:541. (Tr.)

compassion and care of their parents—those most worthy of respect in the life of society—during their illness with perfect respect and filial kindness, showing the exaltedness of humanity.

There is great happiness and joy during an illness which arises from the kindness, pity, and compassion of those around the one who is sick; they reduce the pains of the illness to nothing. The acceptability of the prayers of the sick is of great importance. For the past thirty or forty years, I myself have prayed to be cured of the lumbago from which I suffer. However, I understood that the illness was given to me as an encouragement to prayer. Since prayer cannot be removed through prayer, that is, since prayer cannot remove itself,[10] I understood that the answer to prayers will be obtained in the Hereafter, and that illness is itself a kind of worship, for through illness one realizes one's innate impotence and seeks refuge in the Divine Court. Therefore, although I have prayed for thirty years to be healed and apparently my prayer has not been accepted, it has never occurred to me to abandon the prayer. Because illness is the occasion or reason for prayer; to be cured is not the effect of the prayer. If the All-Wise and Compassionate One bestows healing, He bestows it out of His pure grace.

Furthermore, if prayers are not accepted in the form we desire, it should not be said that they have not been answered. The All-Wise Creator knows better than us; He gives whatever is good for us. Sometimes in our interest He accepts our prayers for our worldly life in the name of our afterlife. In any event, a prayer that acquires sincerity due to an illness and which arises from our

---

[10] Certain illnesses encourage and are the reason for prayer. Therefore, if a prayer causes the termination of the illness, then prayer would annul the reason for it. This cannot be admitted

innate weakness, impotence, humility and need in particular, is very close to being acceptable. Illness is the means to the prayer that is sincere in this way. Both the sick who are religious and believers who look after the sick should make the most of this prayer.

❈ Eighteenth Remedy

*Y*ou who are ill and have abandoned offering thanks and have now taken up complaining! Complaints arise from a right to complain. You have no rights violated, nor have you lost anything which would allow you to complain. Rather, there are numerous thanks that are obligatory for you, but you have not fulfilled them. Without performing your duties towards God Almighty, which are His rights over you, you are complaining as if you are demanding rights in a manner that is not righteous. You cannot look at others who are better off than you in health and complain. You are rather charged with looking at those who are worse than you in health, and offering thanks. If your hand is broken, look at those whose hands have been severed. If you have only one eye, look at those blind, lacking both eyes. And offer thanks to God!

Certainly, no one has the right to consider others as more advantaged than themselves in regard to bounties and to complain. And in tribulations, it is the right of all to consider those who are worse off than themselves, and thus offer thanks. This truth has been explained in a number of places in the *Risale-i Nur* with a simile, a summary of which is as follows:

A person conducts a poor wretch to the top of a minaret. At every step he gives the wretch a different gift, a different bounty. Right at the top of the minaret he gives him the largest gift. Although he deserves thanks and gratitude in return for all those various gifts, the churlish wretch forgets the gifts he has received at each step, or considers them of no importance, and without offering thanks, looks above him and begins to complain, saying: "If only this minaret had been higher, I could have climbed even further. Why isn't it as tall as that mountain over there or that other minaret?" If he begins to complain like this, what great ingratitude this is, what a great wrong!

In the same way, every human being comes into existence from nothing, and without being a rock or a tree or an animal, becomes human. Furthermore, being a Muslim is another great bounty. Most of the time, we enjoy good health and are honored with a great number of bounties. Despite all this, to complain and show impatience because we are not worthy of some bounties due to certain deficiencies pertaining to ourselves, or because we lose them through wrong choices or abuses, or because we were unable to obtain them, and thus to criticize the Divine Lordship, saying, "What have I done to cause this to happen to me?" is a spiritual sickness more disastrous than the physical one. Like fighting with a broken hand, complaint makes illness worse. The sensible person is the one who is proclaimed as,

Those who, when a disaster befalls them, say, "Surely we belong to God (as His creatures and servants), and surely to Him we

are bound to return." (And they act accordingly),

—Al-Baqarah, 2: 156

and shows patience in submission to God Almighty, so that the illness may complete its duty and depart.

✵ Nineteenth Remedy

*A*s a term signifying God's being the Eternally Besought-of-All, while He Himself is in need of nothing, "the All-Beautiful Names" show that all the Names of the All-Gracious One of Majesty are beautiful. Among created beings, the most subtle, the most beautiful, the most comprehensive mirror that reflects God's being the Eternally Besought-of-All is life. The mirror to the beautiful is beautiful. The mirror that shows the beauties of the beautiful becomes beautiful. Just as whatever befalls the mirror through such beauty is good and beautiful, so also whatever befalls life, from the viewpoint of truth, is good, because it exhibits the beautiful imprints of the All-Beautiful Names, which are all good and beautiful.

If life passes monotonously with permanent health and appetite, it becomes a deficient mirror. Indeed, in one respect , it suggests non- existence and nothingness, and causes weariness. It reduces the value of life, and changes the pleasure of life into distress. With the intention of passing their time quickly, out of boredom people let themselves fall into either dissipation or into distractions. They become hostile to their valuable life as if it were a prison sentence, and want to kill it, and make it pass quickly. By contrast, a life that revolves in change and action and different states makes its value felt, and enables us to recognize its importance and pleasure. Even if it is a life of troubles and misfortune, one with such a life does not want life to pass quickly. They make no complaints out of boredom; they do not utter, "Alas! The sun hasn't set yet," or, "It is still night time."

Ask a rich and idle gentleman who is living in the lap of luxury with nothing lacking, "How are you?" You will certainly hear a pathetic reply like, "Time never passes. Let's have a game of backgammon. Or let's find some other distraction to make time pass." Or else you will hear complaints arising from long-term worldly ambitions, like, "I haven't attained this; if only I had done that activity."

Then ask someone struck by disaster or a laborer or a poor man who is in hardship, "How are you?" If they are sensible, they will reply,

> "All thanks be to my Lord, I am well and working. If only the evening did not come so quickly, I could have finished this task! Time passes so quickly, and life goes on without stopping. Certainly, I have troubles and difficulties, but they will pass too. Everything passes quickly."

In effect, such a person is saying how valuable life is and how they regret its passing. This means that they understand the pleasure and value of life which comes with hardship and labor, while ease and health make life bitter and make one desire for it to pass.

You, brother or sister Muslim, who are sick! As is explained convincingly and in detail in some other parts of the *Risale-i Nur*, know that the origin and culture of calamities and evils, and even of sins, is non-existence. As for non-existence, it is evil and darkness. It is because states like continuous ease, silence, inertia, and being sedentary are close to non-existence and nothingness that they make felt the darkness of non- existence and cause distress. As for action and change, they are existence and make existence felt. And existence is pure good, and it is light.

Since this is a reality, your illness has been sent to your body as a guest so that it will carry out many duties like purifying your valuable life, and strengthening and developing it, as well as making other members and faculties of your body turn in assistance towards the part of you that is unwell, and displaying the imprints of various Names of the All-Wise Maker. God willing, the illness will carry out its duties quickly and depart. And it will say to good health,

> "Now you come, and stay permanently in my place, and carry out your duties. This house is yours. Remain here in a good condition."

❖ Twentieth Remedy

*Y*ou who are sick and seeking a remedy for your ills! Illness is of two kinds. One kind is real; the other is imaginary. As for the real kind, the All-Wise Healer of Majesty has stored up in His mighty pharmacy of the earth a remedy for every illness. Without illness, how can those remedies be known and enjoyed? The Religion requires that medicines should be used in treatment, but we should know that their effect and the cure are from God Almighty. It is He Who gives the cure, and it is He Who provides the medicine.

Following the recommendations of skilful, God-conscious doctors is an important form of treatment. For most illnesses arise from abuses, a lack of abstinence, extravagance, vice, dissipation, and indifference and a lack of care. A God-conscious doctor will certainly give advice and orders that are not contrary to Islamic precepts. They will forbid abuses and extravagance, and give consolation. The sick person has confidence in their recommendations and consolation, and the illness wanes, giving a feeling of relief in place of distress.

But when it comes to illnesses that are imaginary, the most effective medicine of all is to give it no importance. The more importance is given to it, the more it grows and swells. If no importance is given, the illness lessens and fades away. The more bees are disturbed, the more they swarm around a person's head, while if they are paid no attention, they disperse. Also, the more attention one pays to a piece of string waving in front of one's eyes in the darkness, the more it disturbs one and causes one to flee from it like a madman. While if you pay it no attention, you can see that it is an ordinary bit of string and not a snake, and you will laugh at your fear and anxiety.

If the groundless worry about one's health continues for a long time, it is transformed into reality. It is an evil ailment for the nervous and those given to groundless fears and worries; such people make a mountain out of a molehill and their morale is destroyed. In particular, if they encounter unkind and unfair "half" doctors, their worries are provoked and increase. If they are rich, they lose their wealth, or else they lose their wits, or their health.

❖ Twenty-First Remedy

You, brother or sister in faith, who are sick! You are suffering physical pain because of your illness, but a significant spiritual pleasure which will remove the effect of your physical pain surrounds you. For if you have a father, mother, or relatives, their most pleasurable compassion towards you, which you have long forgotten, will be awakened and you will see again their kind looks which you received in childhood. In addition, the friends around you who have remained veiled and hidden will look again towards you with love through the attraction of illness. In the face of these, your physical pain is infinitesimal. Also, those whom you serve proudly and from whom you try to receive appreciation now serve you kindly due to your illness, and thus you have become a master of your masters. Furthermore, since you have attracted towards yourself the fellow feeling and human tenderness of people, you have found many helpful friends and kind companions who expect nothing in return. Again, you have received from your illness the order to rest from many exhausting duties, and you are taking a rest. Certainly, in the face of these spiritual pleasures, your minor pain should lead you to thanks, not to complaint.

Twenty-Second Remedy

*Y*ou, brother or sister in faith, who suffer a severe illness such as paralysis! Firstly, I give you the good news that for believers paralysis is regarded as blessed. I have long heard this from saintly people, but I did not know the reason. Now, one reason occurs to me as follows:

In order to obtain the approval and good pleasure of God Almighty, and to be saved from the great dangers that this world poses to the spiritual life, and to attain eternal happiness, the people of God have chosen to follow two principles:

- *The first* is contemplation of death. Thinking of the world as transitory and realizing that they too are transient guests in the world who have many duties, they work for the eternal life in this way.

- *The second*: In order to be saved from the dangers of the carnal, evil-commanding soul and blind passions, they have tried to kill the evil-commanding soul through austerity, religious exercises, and asceticism.

And you, my brother or sister, who have lost the health of half your body! Without choosing to do so, you have been given these two principles, which are the cause of happiness, so that your body continually warns you against the fleeting nature of the world and reminds you that humans are mortal. The world cannot drown you anymore, nor can heedlessness close your eyes. And certainly, the carnal, evil-commanding soul cannot deceive someone in the state of half a person by vile lusts and animal appetites; that person is quickly saved from the trials of the evil-commanding soul.

Thus, through belief in and submission to God and reliance on Him, a believer can benefit in a short time from a severe illness like paralysis, rather than undergoing the severe trials of the saints. Thus an illness that is so severe becomes an exceedingly modest exchange for these gains.

✸ Twenty-Third Remedy

You who are ill and unhappy, alone and a stranger! While your isolation and exile together with your illness arouse sympathy in the hardest hearts and attract kindness and compassion to you, certainly they will also attract the All-Compassionate Creator's compassion towards you, which is certain to be a substitute for the sympathy and compassion of everything else. It is He Who presents Himself to us at the start of all but one of the *suras* of the Qur'an with the Attributes of "All-Merciful and All-Compassionate." Through one gleam of His Compassion, He causes all mothers to nurture their young with wonderful tenderness, and through one manifestation of His Mercy every spring, He fills the face of the earth with bounties. Also, with all its wonders, Paradise, which is the abode of eternal happiness, constitutes a single manifestation of His Mercy. Thus, your relation to Him through belief, your recognition of Him and entreating Him through the voice of helplessness that is found in your illness, and your loneliness in exile will surely attract His mercy towards you.

Since He exists and He looks to you, everything exists for you. Those who are truly alone and in exile are those who have no relation to Him through belief and submission, or who attach no importance to that relation.

✸ Twenty-Fourth Remedy

*Y*ou who tend innocent, sick children or the elderly who are like innocent children! Before you is an important commodity for the Hereafter. Carry out these tasks with zeal and endeavor! In the illnesses of innocent children there are many instances of wisdom pertaining to their worldly life. For instance, their illnesses are like exercises and drills for their delicate bodies, and the inoculations and training of the Lord, so that they may be able to withstand the tumults and upheavals of the world in the future. As is accepted by verifying scholars, like expiations for sins in adults, the illnesses of innocent children are also inoculations which will serve their spiritual life, their spiritual purification and development in the future or in the Hereafter. In addition, the merits ensuing from such illnesses are recorded in the notebook of the good deeds of the parents, and particularly of the mother who, out of compassion, prefers the health of her child to her own.

As for looking after the elderly, it is accurately reported from our Prophet, upon him be peace and blessings, and has been established by many historical events, that in addition to bringing mighty rewards, receiving the prayers of the elderly, and especially that of parents, and making their hearts happy and serving them faithfully is the means to happiness both in this world and in the Hereafter.[11] And there are many experiences that establish that a child who perfectly obeys his elderly parents will receive the same treatment from his or her children, and that a child who wounds his or her parents will not only be punished in the Hereafter, but will also be subject to many disasters in this world. Not only looking after relatives who are elderly or innocent children, but also serving willingly any believing sick person, especially if that one is in need of us—since there is true brotherhood coming from belief—is a requirement of being a Muslim.

✸ Twenty-Fifth Remedy

*Y*ou, brother and sister Muslims, who are ill! If you desire a most beneficial, truly pleasurable, and sacred medicine, which is the cure for every illness, develop your belief! That is, through repentance and seeking God's forgiveness for your sins, and the five daily Prayers, and other duties of worship, apply to your illnesses belief—that sacred cure—and the medicine it provides.

Indeed, due to the love of this world and attachment to it, it is as if the worldly people have a sick worldly existence as big as the world. We have convincingly explained in many parts of the *Risale-i Nur* that belief immediately heals that sick existence, which, like the world itself, is subject to the blows of death and separation and "riddled" with wounds and bruises. I cut short the discussion here not to weary you.

---

[11] *al-Bukhari*, "Adab" 1–6,; *Muslim*, "Birr" 1–6, 9, 10; *at-Tirmidhi*, "Da'awat" 110.

As for the medicine of belief, it shows its effect when you carry out your religious obligations as far as is possible. Heedlessness, dissipation, carnal desires, and religiously forbidden amusements prevent the effectiveness of that remedy. Since illness removes heedlessness, reduces the appetites, and prevents one from partaking in religiously unlawful pleasures, take advantage of it. Apply the sacred medicines and lights of true belief through repentance, seeking God's forgiveness, and prayers, and supplications.

May Almighty God restore you to health and make your illnesses expiation for your sins.

Amen. Amen. Amen.

They say: "All praise and gratitude are for God, Who has guided us to this. If God had not guided us, we would certainly not have found the right way. The Messengers of our Lord did indeed come with the truth."

—Al-A'rāf, 7:43

"All-Glorified are You. We have no knowledge save what You have taught us. Surely You are the All-Knowing, the All-Wise".

—Al-Baqarah, 2:32

O God! Bestow blessings on our master Muhammad ﷺ,
the medicine for hearts and their cure,
the good health of bodies and their healing,
the light of eyes and their light, and
on his Family and Companions,
and bestow on them peace.

PART TWO

Treatise for the Elderly

Being the **26th** Flash from the Flashes Collection of *Risale-i Nur.* Volume 3

This Flash consists of twenty-six hopes, lights, and solaces.

Hope and solace for the elderly

NOTE: The reason why, at the beginning of each Hope, I have written of my sorrows and afflictions in a way that may sadden you is to show the extraordinary efficacy of the remedies proceeding from the All-Wise Qur'an.

This *Flash*, which is about the elderly, may have been unable to attain fluency due to certain reasons, such as those that follow:

THE FIRST: Since it has been generally based on my own experiences and written in a mood that arises from recalling those former times, it was not possible to attain a sequence in expression.

THE SECOND: Since it was written rapidly after the early morning Prayer, when I felt fatigued, there is some confusion in expression.

THE THIRD: There was not always somebody with me to write, and the scribe who accompanied me had four or five other duties concerning the *Risale-i Nur*. Since we therefore could not find enough time to revise it thoroughly, there is a certain disorder.

THE FOURTH: Both the scribe and I were exhausted after its completion, and felt compelled to be content with a superficial revision of the wording without considering the expression adequately. Because of this, there may naturally be errors of expression. We request that the magnanimous elderly will overlook my errors of expression and as Divine Mercy does not leave empty the hands of the blessed elderly which are opened towards It,[1] we hope that they will include us in their prayers when they open their hands towards the Divine Court.

---

[1] at-Tabarani, *al-Majma' al-Awsat*, 5:270; al-Haythami, *Majma' az-Zawa'id*, 10: 149. (Tr.)

In the Name of God, the Merciful, the Compassionate.

Kaf. Ha. Ya. 'Ayn. Sad. A mention of your Lord's mercy to His servant Zachariah: When he invoked his Lord with a call in secret, saying: "My Lord! My bones have grown feeble and my head glistens with gray hair from old age, and, my Lord, I have never been unblessed in my prayer to You."

—Maryam, 19:1-4

✹ First Hope

Respected elderly brothers and sisters who have reached the age of maturity: Like you, I am elderly. Out of the desire to share with you the lights of consolation they contain, I will write the Hopes which I have, from time to time, found in my old age and some of my experiences. Of course, the lights I have seen and the doors of hope I have encountered have been seen and opened according to my defective and confused capacity. God willing, your pure and sincere dispositions will make the lights I have seen shine more brightly and strengthen the hopes I have found.

The source, spring, and fount of the hopes and lights to follow is belief (in God and the other pillars of faith).

✹ Second Hope

One autumn day when old age was upon me, at about the time of the afternoon Prayer, I was looking at the world from a high mountain and I became overwhelmed by a piteous, mournful and, in some sense, dark mood or state of mind. I saw that I had become old. The day also had grown old, and so had the year; and so too had the world. All those instances of old age made me feel that the time of departure from the world and separation from those I loved had drawn close, and my own old age shook me severely. Suddenly Divine Mercy unfolded in such a way that it changed that piteous sadness and separation into a powerful hope and radiant light of solace. I affirm to you who are elderly like me: the All-Compassionate Creator presents Himself to us in a hundred places in the wise Qur'an as *the All-Merciful and the All-Compassionate.* He is always sending His mercy to the aid of the living creatures on the earth which seek it. Every year He sends the spring, which He fills with innumerable bounties and gifts from the Unseen, to us, who are needy of provision, and manifests His mercy abundantly proportionate to our innate weakness and impotence. Thus, the Mercy[2] of our All-Compassionate Creator is the greatest hope and most powerful light in our old age. We can find this Mercy by forming a connection with and adhering to the All-Merciful through belief and by obeying Him by performing the daily Prayers.

Third Hope

When I awoke in the morning of old age from the sleep of the night of youth, I looked at myself and saw that my life was hurrying towards the grave as though speeding down a slope. As Niyazi Misri[3] said,

---

[2] The things concerning or belonging to God Almighty are sometimes initiated with capital letters and sometimes with small ones. For example, in this paragraph "mercy" is initiated either with a capital letter or with a small one. If it refers to God's Name or Attribute, it is initiated with a capital letter, but if it refers to a manifestation of that Name or Attribute, it is initiated with a small letter. (Tr.)

[3] Mehmet Niyazi Misri (1617-1694). He was born in Malatya, Turkey, and died in the island of Limni in the Agean Sea. He was a Sufi *shaykh*, poet, and scholar. *Ilmihali Tariqat* ("The Principles of the Sufi Way"), *Mawadi al-*

Each day a stone from the building
of my life falls to the ground;
The soul slumbers in heedlessness and
is unaware that its building is in ruins!

my body, the dwelling of my spirit, was decaying, with a stone of it crumbling every day. Having felt this, the hopes and ambitions that had bound me strongly to the world began to be broken off. I felt that the time of separation from my many friends and those I loved was drawing near. I searched for an ointment for that very deep and apparently incurable spiritual wound, but I could find none. Again like Niyazi Misri I said:

While my heart desired permanence,
God, the Truth,
judged the mortality of my body;
I am afflicted with an incurable ill;
how pitiful it is that Luqman is unaware of it!

Then suddenly the light and intercession of the glorious Prophet, upon him be peace and blessings, who is the voice, model, embodiment, herald, and representative of Divine Mercy, and the gift of guidance he had brought to humankind became a good ointment for that wound which I had supposed to be incurable.

Respected elderly men and women who feel their old age as I do! We are leaving; there is no use in deceiving ourselves. Even if we close our eyes to it, we will not be allowed to remain here. There is mobilization. The land of the Intermediate Realm of the grave, which appears to us as dark and as the land of eternal

---

'Irfan ("The Tables of Esoteric Knowledge"), and *Tevhid Risalesi* (A Treatise of God's Oneness") are among his most famous works. (Tr.)

separation because of the delusions that arise from heedlessness and in part from the people of misguidance, is the meeting place of friends. It is the realm where we will meet with, foremost, God's Beloved, upon him be peace and blessings, and with all our friends.

We are going to the world of the one who for one thousand three hundred and fifty years, has been the ruler of hundreds of millions of people, and the trainer of their spirits, the teacher of their minds, and the beloved of their hearts. According to the rule, "The cause is like the doer," the equivalent of the merit that his whole Community gains every day through its good deeds is added to his notebook of good deeds. He is the means for the realization of the exalted Divine purposes in the universe and the increase of the value of beings. As recorded in authentic Traditions and discovered by saints of spiritual discovery, when he came into the world, he exclaimed, "My Community! My Community!"[4] He will also hasten to the aid of his Community with the loftiest self-sacrifice and through his intercession when everyone will consider only themselves in the Place of Supreme Gathering in the other world, and again he will exclaim, "My Community! My Community!"[5] We are going to a world that is illuminated by this sun and by the stars of countless saints and purified scholars.

The means of being entitled to that person's intercession, profiting from his light, and being saved from the darkness of the Intermediate Realm is to follow his noble example or way (*Sunnah*).

---

[4] as-Suyuti, *al-Khasa'is al-Kubra*, 1:80, 85. (Tr.)
[5] *al-Bukhari*, "Tawhid" 36; *Muslim*, "Iman" 326. (Tr.)

✸ Fourth Hope

*W*hen I stepped into old age, my physical health, which perpetuates heedlessness, was broken. Old age and illness attacked me together in unison. They continuously disturbed me, causing unceasing trouble. I had nothing binding me to the world, no family, children, or possessions. I saw the fruit of my life's capital, which I had wasted through the giddiness of youth, to be only sins and errors. Crying out like Niyazi Misri, I said:

> I had concluded no trade;
> the capital of life was all wasted away;
> I found the road only to find the caravan
> had moved on while I had been unaware.

> Lamenting, I too set off, all alone, a stranger,
> With eyes weeping, heart in anguish,
> mind bewildered and unaware.

I was in exile at the time. I felt a despairing sorrow, a deep regret, a longing for assistance. All at once, the Qur'an of miraculous expression came to my aid. It opened for me such a powerful door of hope and offered me such a light of true consolation that it could have removed any despair and darkness that was a hundred times more intense than mine.

Respected elderly men and women whose interests in the world have begun to cease when the ties that bind them to this world are gradually broken! Is it possible that the Maker of Majesty, Who has created this world as a most perfectly ordered city or palace, would not meet or speak to His most important guests and friends in that palace? Since He knowingly made this palace and ordered and decorated it purposefully, certainly—just as the one who makes something knows—the One Who knows will speak. And since He has made this palace and city as a fine guesthouse and place of trade for us, He will certainly have a book that demonstrates His relations for us and what He desires from us.

The most perfect of such sacred Books is the Qur'an of miraculous expression. It is a miracle in forty respects and at every instant is on the tongues of at least a hundred million people. It diffuses light, and every letter of it provides at least ten merits and rewards, and sometimes ten thousand fruits of Paradise and lights in the Intermediate Realm, and sometimes—due to the meaning and importance of the Night of Destiny and Power—thirty thousand. It also provides the fruit of Paradise and light for the Intermediate Realm of the grave. There is no book in the universe to compete with it in these respects and no one can put one forward. As this Qur'an we hold is the Word of the All-Majestic Creator of the heavens and earth, having issued from His absolute Lordship, supreme Divinity, and all-encompassing Mercy, and is His decree and a source of His mercy—adhere to it. In it is a cure for every ill, a light for every veil and kind of darkness, and a hope for every instance of despair.

The key to this eternal treasury is belief and submission to God, listening to the Qur'an and accepting and reciting it.

❖ Fifth Hope

Once, at the onset of my old age, my spirit sought ease in solitude on Mount Joshua (Yusha Tepesi) up the Bosphorus in Istanbul. One day on that high hill, I looked around at the broad horizon, and saw an extremely pathetic scene of decay and separation through the warning of old age. I took a look from the high position of the forty-fifth branch, that is, the forty-fifth year, of the tree of my life to my life's lower levels. I saw that down on each of the lower branches, in each year, there were numerous corpses of those I knew and loved, and to whom I was somehow related. Thinking of the friends who had left, with truly pitiful sorrow that arose from separation, I groaned like Fuzuli of Baghdad:[6]

> As I recall your company I weep,
> So long as there is breath in this dry body of mine, I cry out …

So saying, I sought solace, a light, a door of hope. All at once, the light of belief in the Hereafter came to my aid, offering an inextinguishable light, an indestructible hope. It is as follows:

Brothers and sisters who are elderly like me! As there is the Hereafter and it is everlasting, and it is a realm much better than this world, and as the One Who has created us is both All-Wise and All-Compassionate, we should not complain of or regret our old age. On the contrary, since old age is a sign of reaching the age of maturity in belief and worship, and signals a discharge from the duties of life and departure for the world of mercy in order to rest, we should be pleased with it.

A *hadith* says that one hundred and twenty-four thousand Prophets, who are the most eminent and distinguished among

---

[6] Mehmed Fuzuli (1490-1556). One of the greatest poets of Turkish literature. He lived in Iraq and wrote many works both in verse and in prose. His *Divan* ("Collection of Poems"), which he wrote in Turkish, Persian, and Arabic is the most famous among his works. *Laylawu Majnun* ("Layla and Majnun"), *Tarjuma-i Hadith-i Arbain* ("The Translation of the Forty Hadiths"), and *Hadiqat as-Su'ada'* ("The Garden of the Holy Ones") are among his most famous works. (Tr.)

humanity, have been sent.[7] All of these Prophets, based on Divine Revelation and their own spiritual observation, unanimously and in complete agreement gave news that the Hereafter does exist, that human beings will be sent there, and that the Creator will bring it as He promised. In addition, one hundred and twenty-four million saints, with spiritual illumination, discovery, and observation have confirmed the reports of the Prophets with the degree of certainty arising from knowledge, and testified to the existence of the Hereafter. Also, all the Names of the All-Wise Maker, through their manifestations in this world, show the absolutely necessary existence of and necessitate an everlasting realm. For example, the Eternal Power, Which every spring restores to life innumerable corpses of dead trees on the face of the earth with the command of *"Be!" and it is*, and Which revives hundreds of thousands of species of plants and animals as samples of the resurrection of the dead, most clearly necessitates the existence of the Hereafter. Likewise, the infinite, Eternal Wisdom, Which allows nothing to be in vain or purposeless, and the Eternal Mercy and Perpetual Favor, Which, with perfect compassion and in an extremely wonderful fashion, provides the sustenance of all living beings that are in need of it, and for a brief time in spring allow them to display their manifold varieties of adornment and decoration, require the Hereafter. Furthermore, the human being is the most perfect fruit of the universe and its Creator's most beloved creature, and of all beings the human is the most closely and deeply connected and concerned with the other beings in the universe. The intense, unshakeable, and constant love of eternity and ambition for permanence that are innate in human nature prove the existence of a permanent realm,

---

[7] Ahmad ibn Hanbal, *al-Musnad*, 5:265; Ibn Hibban, *as-Sahih*, 2:77. (Tr.)

an everlasting abode of happiness that will follow this transient world, so decisively that they necessitate the acceptance of the Hereafter with the same certainty that we accept the existence of this world.[8]

Since one of the most important things the wise Qur'an teaches us is belief in the Hereafter, and since this belief is so powerful and it provides such hope and solace that if a single person were overwhelmed by old age a hundred thousand times over, the consolation arising from this belief would be sufficient to face it, then surely we who are elderly should say, "All praise be to God for perfect belief," and love our old age.

Sixth Hope

Once during my distressing surveillance, having preferred seclusion, I was alone on the top of Pine Mountain (Çam Dağı) in the Barla plateau (in the province of Isparta). I was in need of a light in my isolation. Alone one night on the small

---

[8] The ease of reporting something which definitely exists and the extreme difficulty in denying it may be seen in the following comparison: if one person says, "There is a wonderful garden on earth, the trees of which have fruits that are cans of milk," and another says, "There isn't," the one claiming it proves his or her claim only by pointing out its place or some of its fruits or a single member of it. Whereas, the one denying it has to scan and show the whole face of the earth. In just the same way, even if we ignore the hundreds of thousands of signs, fruits, and marks of Paradise which those who report its existence have pointed out, the testimony of two truthful witnesses to the truth of their report is sufficient. But in order to prove his denial, the one who denies it has to scan the limitless universe and infinite, unending time, and demonstrate its non- existence. And so, my elderly brothers and sisters, understand just how powerful is belief in the Hereafter.

platform at the top of a tall pine on the summit of that high mountain, old age recalled to me three or four separations, one within another. As described in The Sixth Letter (included in *The Letters*), the melancholy sound of the rustling trees on that lonely, silent, remote night burdened me greatly in my exile in old age. Old age prompted the following thought: Just as the daylight has changed into this sepulchral black and the world has put on its black shroud, so too the daytime of your life will turn into night, and the daytime of the world turn into the night of the Intermediate Realm of the grave, and the summertime of life into the winter night-time of death. It whispered this in my heart's ear. My soul was then obliged to respond:

True, I am far from my native land, but being separated from and mourning all those who are now dead, whom I loved during my fifty years of life, is a far more grievous and sorrowful separation than exile from my country. Furthermore, I am drawing close to a much more sorrowful and painful exile than the melancholy exile of the night and the mountain: old age informs me that I am approaching the time of separation from the world altogether.

I then sought a light, a hope, from these sorrowful separations, one within the other. Suddenly belief in God came to my aid and offered such companionship that even if the layered desolation in which I found myself had increased a thousand times, its consolation would have been sufficient.

Elderly men and women! Since we have a Compassionate Creator, there can be no exile for us. Since He exists, everything exists for us. Since He exists and has angels, the world is not empty. Lonely mountains and empty deserts are full of God Almighty's servants. Apart from His conscious servants, His stones and trees also become like familiar friends when viewed through His light and on His account. They may converse with us and give us contentment.

Evidence and testimonies to the number of beings in the universe and to the number of the letters of this vast book of the universe affirm the existence of our All-Compassionate, All-Munificent, All-Intimate, and All-Loving Creator, Maker, and Protector. They show us His Mercy to the number of the members of the living creatures' members, and of the provision and favors they enjoy, all of which are the instruments of His Compassion, Mercy, and Grace, and point the way to His Court. The most acceptable intercessor at His Court is impotence, weakness, and neediness. And the greatest time of impotence, weakness, and neediness is old age. So we should not resent old age, which is an acceptable intercessor at this Court, but welcome it.

Seventh Hope

Once at the onset of old age when the laughter of the Old or Former Said was changing into the weeping of the New Said, some worldly-minded people in Ankara, supposing me to be still the Old Said, invited me there, and I went. At the close of autumn I climbed to the top of the city fort, which was dilapidated, and far more aged than me. It seemed to me as if it were formed by petrified historical events. The old age of the season of the year together with my old age, the fort's old age, humankind's old age, the old age of the glorious Ottoman State, and the demise of the sultanate representing caliphate, and the world's old age all caused me to look in the most sorrowful, piteous, and melancholy state from that lofty fort to the valleys of the past and the mountains of the future. I found myself in an utterly dark state of mind in Ankara, encompassed by four or five layers of the darkness's of old age, one within the other, and I sought a light, a solace, a hope.

As I looked to the right, that is, to the past, to find solace, it appeared to me in the form of the vast graveyard of my father and forefathers and the human race, causing me gloom rather than consolation. Seeking a cure I looked to the future on the left. It appeared as a huge, dark graveyard for myself, my contemporaries, and future generations, giving horror in place of relief and solace. Frightened in the face of what was to the left and right, I looked to the present time. To my heedless and historical eye it appeared as a coffin bearing my half-dead, suffering corpse, which was desperately struggling as if dying. Then, despairing from that direction as well, I raised my head and looked to the top of the tree of my life, and there was my corpse: it rested at the top of the tree and was watching me. Feeling horror from this direction too, I lowered my head, looking to the foot of the tree of my life, to its roots. I saw that the dust of my bones underfoot had mixed with the dust of my creation. That too provided no cure; it doubled my pain.

Then I felt forced to look behind me. I saw that this temporary world, which has no foundation, was revolving through the valleys of nothingness and the darkness of non- existence. I had been seeking a medicine for my pain, but this view only aggravated it. Seeing no good in that direction, I looked in front of me, I cast my eye ahead. I saw the entrance of a grave plain to view, right in my path, open and staring at me, its mouth wide open. The highway behind it led to eternity and the convoys traveling it caught my eye. And all that I have as my support and defense in the face of the horrors that come from these six directions is only a limited, insignificant willpower. Since that willpower, which is the sole human defense against those innumerable enemies and harmful things, is defective, short-range, and feeble, with no power to create, it is capable of nothing apart from being something receptive and committing. It can neither turn back and enter the past so that it can silence the sorrows that arise from there nor can it penetrate the future so that it can prevent the fears that come from there. I saw that my pains and ambitions concerning the past and future were to no avail.

Even as I was struggling with the horror, isolation, darkness and despair coming from these six directions, the lights of belief which shine in the heaven of the Qur'an of miraculous expression suddenly came to my aid. They lit up and illuminated those six directions to such a degree that if the horrors and darkness I had seen increased a hundredfold, the lights would still have been sufficient to dispel them. One by one they changed all these horrors into comfort and isolation into companionship. It was as follows:

Belief rent asunder the desolate view of the past as a vast graveyard and showed it with utter certainty to be a familiar and enlightened gathering of friends.

Belief showed the future, which appears in the form of a huge graveyard to heedless eyes, certainly to be a banquet of the All-Merciful in delightful palaces of happiness.

Belief rent the view of the present time as a coffin, as it appears to heedless eyes, and showed it with certainty to be a place of trade for the Hereafter and a splendid guesthouse of the All-Merciful.

Belief showed with certainty that the only fruit at the top of the tree of life was not a corpse, as it appears to heedless eyes, but that my spirit, which was created for eternal life and endowed with potential to gain eternal happiness, has left its worn-out home to travel through the stars.

Through its meaning and content, belief showed that my bones and the dust which was the source of my creation were not worthless dust trampled underfoot, but that the soil was the door to Divine Mercy and a veil before the hall of Paradise.

Belief also showed through the Qur'an that the world, which had appeared to my heedless eye as revolving behind me through the valleys of nothingness and the darkness of non- existence, consists of missives of the Eternally Besought-of-All and pages of the embroideries of the Divine glorification of God. When they (these missives and pages, that is, all the existent things and happenings in the world) have completed their tasks, displaying their content and meanings, they depart the world one after the other, leaving their results in existence in their place. With complete certainty the true nature of the world is made known.

Through the light of the Qur'an belief showed that the grave which is looking at me from a certain distance with eyes wide open is not the mouth of a well, but the door to the world of light, and that the highway stretching to eternity beyond the grave leads not to nothingness and non-existence but to existence and a realm of light, and eternal happiness. Since belief has shown this truth with convincing certainty, it is both a cure and ointment for my afflictions.

Furthermore, in place of a very minor ability to choose and implement, belief gives that limited human faculty of willpower a document through which it may rely on an infinite Power and be connected to a limitless Mercy in the face of these innumerable enemies and veils of darkness. Indeed, belief itself is that document in the hand of human willpower. Though this human instrument of willpower is in itself both short-range, feeble, and deficient, yet—just as when a soldier uses his limited capacities on behalf of the state, he performs duties far exceeding those capacities—through belief, if that limited willpower is used in the name of God Almighty and in His cause , it may also gain a paradise as broad as five hundred years of walking.

Belief takes from the body the reins of the willpower, which cannot penetrate the past or the future, and hands them over to the heart and spirit. Since the sphere of the life of the spirit and heart is not restricted to the present time as the body is, and since it encompasses a great many years from the past and a great many years from the future, the willpower no longer becomes limited and acquires universality. Just as through the power of belief it can enter the deepest valleys of the past and remove the darkness of the sorrows that arise from the past, so too through the light of belief it can rise as far as the farthest mountains of the future, and remove the apprehensions and anxieties that arise from there.

And so, my elderly brothers and sisters who, like me, are suffering the hardships of old age! Since, all praise be to God, we are believers, and belief contains so many light-diffusing, delightful, pleasant, and satisfying treasures; and since our old age drives us even further into the contents of those treasures, then, surely, rather than complaining about old age that is accompanied by belief, we should be offering endless thanks for it.

❊ Eighth Hope

At a time when grey hairs, the sign of old age, were appearing on my head, I returned to Istanbul from captivity as a prisoner of war (in Russia) after the turmoil of the First World War, and this made the deep sleep of youth even heavier. In addition to the great celebrity and honor accorded to me, the kind treatment and attention far exceeding my due that I received from everyone, from the caliph, the *shaykhul-Islam*, and the commander in chief of the army to the students of religious schools, the intoxication of youth, and the mood produced by my position made the sleep of youth so heavy that I saw the world as perpetual and myself cemented in it as if there were no longer death.

Then, one day in the holy month of Ramadan, I went to Bayazid Mosque in Istanbul to listen to the sincere reciters of the Qur'an. Through the tongues of the reciters, the Qur'an of miraculous expression was proclaiming with its exalted heavenly address the decree,

"Every soul is bound to taste death."

—Āl ʿImrān, 3: 185

which most powerfully declares the inevitable death of the human being and of all living creatures. It entered my ear, and established itself in the very center of my heart, shattering the extremely thick layers of my sleep of heedlessness and intoxication. I went out of the mosque. Because of the stupor of the sleep, which had for so long settled in my head in which now a tempest was raging and a fire was burning producing smoke, for several days I saw myself as a boat which had lost its course. Every time I looked in the mirror, the grey hairs told me, "Be careful!" And so the reality showed itself through the warnings of my grey hairs.

I noticed that my youth, which had so captivated me with its pleasures and in which I had so trusted, was saying farewell to me, and this worldly life in which I was so lovingly involved was beginning to fade; the world which I so loved and with which I was closely connected was seeing me off, warning me that I would be leaving this guesthouse. It was itself, while bidding farewell, preparing to depart. From the encompassing content of the verse, *Every soul is bound to taste death*, the following meanings were unfolding in my heart: humankind is a soul—it will die in order to be resurrected; the earth is a soul—it will die in order to assume an eternal form; and the world too is a soul—it will die in order to assume the form of the Hereafter.

So, while in this state, I considered my situation. I saw that youth, which is the mine of pleasures, was going away, being replaced by old age—the source of sorrow. Life, which shines so brightly, was departing, and death, which is apparently dark and terrifying, was preparing to take its place. The lovable world, which is thought to be perpetual and is the beloved of the heedless, was hastening to its demise.

In order to delude myself and plunge my mind into heedlessness once more, I considered the pleasures of the social position I enjoyed in Istanbul, which was far exceeding my due, but it was of no use at all. All the regard, attention, and consolation of people could only attend me as far as the door of the grave, which was so near me; there it would be extinguished. And since I saw a repugnant hypocrisy, cold pretension, self-adulation, and temporary stupefaction under the embellished veil of glory and renown, which is the greatest aim of those who chase celebrity, I understood that these things which had deluded me until then could provide no solace for me and that there was no light to be found in them.

I again turned to the reciters in the Bayazid Mosque in order to hear the heavenly teaching of the Qur'an and to be awakened once more. Then from its exalted instruction I heard glad tidings through such sacred decrees as *And give glad tidings to those who believe...*

Through the radiation provided by the Qur'an, I sought consolation, hope, and light, not beyond but within the matters that had provoked in me horror, desolation and despair. A hundred thousand thanks be to God Almighty, I had found the cure within the affliction itself, I had found the light within the darkness itself, and I had found the solace within the horror itself.

Firstly, I looked in the face of death, which terrifies everyone and is imagined as being the most terrible thing. Through the light of the Qur'an I saw that although death's veil is black, dark, and ugly, for believers its true face is luminous and beautiful. We have convincingly expressed this truth in several parts of the *Risale-i Nur*. For instance, as we explained in the Eighth Word and the Twentieth Letter, death is not extinction and eternal separation; it is rather the introduction to eternal life, its beginning. It is a rest from the hardships of life's duties, a demobilization. It is a change of residence. It is meeting with the caravan of one's friends who have already migrated to the Intermediate World of the grave, and so on. I saw death's true, beautiful face through realities such as these. It was not with fear but with a certain yearning that I looked at the face of death. Indeed, in a sense, it was with yearning, and I understood some meaning of the Sufis' "contemplation of death."

Then I looked at my departed youth, which had been spent in heedlessness—the youth which infatuates everyone and whose departure makes them weep. I saw that within its beautiful embellished garb was the ugliest, most drunken and stupefied face. Had I not learnt its true nature, in return for intoxicating and amusing me for a few years. If I remained in the world a hundred years, it would have caused me to weep that long. One such person lamented,

> "If only one day my youth had returned, I would have told it
> of the woes old age has brought me."

Indeed, elderly people who, like that person, do not know the true nature of youth, think of their own youth, and weep with regret and longing. But youth spent in worship, good works, and trade for the Hereafter by believers with sound minds and hearts is the most powerful means of earning and the most agreeable and pleasant means of doing good works. For those who know their religious duties and do not misspend their youth, it is a precious and enjoyable Divine favor. When it is not spent in uprightness, modesty, and God-consciousness, youth poses numerous risks. When unrestrained, it ruins eternal happiness and the life in this world. Indeed, in return for the pleasures of a few years' youth, many years of grief and sorrow are caused in old age.

Since youth is harmful for most people, we elderly people should thank God that we have been saved from its dangers and harm. Like everything else, the pleasures of youth are transitory. If youth has been spent in worship and good works, its fruits remain perpetually in place and will be the means of gaining youth in eternal life.

Next, I looked at the world, which most people love with deep attachment. Through the light of the Qur'an, I saw that there are three universal worlds, one within the other:

- *The first* relates to the Divine Names; it is a mirror to them.

- *The second* relates to the Hereafter; it is an arable field for it.

- *The third* relates to worldly people; it is the playground of the heedless.

Moreover, everyone has his own particular world within this world. It is as if there are worlds, one within the other, equal to the number of human beings. But the pillar of everyone's private world is their own life. When their bodies are destroyed, their world collapses on their head, and it is doomsday for them. Since the heedless do not realize that their world has such a nature, which is bound for such speedy destruction, they suppose it to be perpetual as the general world appears to be and adore it. I thought to myself, "I too have a private world that will quickly collapse like the worlds of other people. What value does this private world of mine, this short life of mine, have?"

Through the light of the Qur'an, I saw that both for myself and everyone else this world is a temporary market place set up on the road for the passers-by to shop in, a guesthouse which is every day filled and emptied, an ever-renewed notebook of the Eternal Inscriber, in which He continuously writes and erases; every spring is a gilded letter of His and every summer a well-composed ode. It is formed of mirrors that reflect the ever-renewed manifestations of the All-Majestic Maker's Names; it is a seedbed of the Hereafter, a flowerbed of Divine Mercy, and a temporary workshop producing tablets that will be displayed in the Realm of Eternity.

I offer a hundred thousand thanks to the Creator of Majesty, Who has made the world in this way. I understood that while humankind has been endowed with love for the beautiful, inner faces of the world, which look to the Hereafter and Divine Names, many have wasted that love on its transient, ugly, harmful, heedless face, and so realized the meaning of the *hadith*,

"Love of this world is the source of all errors."[9]

And so, elderly brothers and sisters, I realized this truth through the light of the wise Qur'an, and the warnings of my old age and belief opened my eyes; I have demonstrated this with decisive proofs in several parts of the *Risale-I Nur*. I have found a true solace, powerful hope, and radiant light. I am happy that I am old; and I am glad that my youth is gone. You do likewise: do not weep, but offer thanks. Since there is belief and since the truth is thus, it is the heedless who should weep and the misguided who should lament.

❈ Ninth Hope

*O*n the First World War, I was in the distant province of Kosturma in north-eastern Russia as a prisoner of war. There was a small mosque there belonging to the Tatars beside the famous Volga River. I became weary among my friends, the other officers. I wished for solitude, yet I could not stroll about outside without permission. Then they allowed me out on bail to the Tatar quarter, to that small mosque on the banks of the Volga. I would stay in the mosque alone. Spring was close. I would be awake for quite long times during the long, long nights of that northern land. The pathetic splashing of the Volga and the moving patter of the rain and the sad blowing of the wind during

---

[9] al-Bayhaqi, *Shu'ab al-Iman*, 7:338; al-Mundhiri, *at-Targhib wat-Tarhib*, 3:178. (Tr.)

those dark nights in that dark exile temporarily awakened me from the deep sleep of heedlessness. I did not yet consider myself old, but those who experienced the World War were considered to be old. For those were the days that, as though manifesting the meaning of the verse,

"A Day which will turn the children gray-headed."

—Al-Muzzammil, 73: 17

made even children old. So, although I was forty years old, I felt as if I were eighty. In those long, dark nights during that sorrowful exile and melancholy, I felt despair of life and for my homeland. In the face of my powerlessness and loneliness, my hope failed.

Then, while I was in that state, the wise Qur'an came to my aid. My tongue uttered,

"God is sufficient for us; and how excellent a guardian is He."

—Āl 'Imrān, 3:173

and weeping, my heart cried out:

I am a stranger, I am lonely and weak, and I am powerless:
I beg mercy, ask forgiveness, and
I cry for help from Your Court, O my God!

And, thinking of my old friends in my homeland, and imagining myself dying in exile there, like Niyazi Misri, I said as follows:

Renouncing the world's grief,
Taking flight into nothingness,
Flying constantly with ardor,

I call in each breath, Friend! Friend!
My spirit was searching for its friends.

In any case, my neediness and weakness became such powerful intercessors and means at the Divine Court in that long, melancholy, pitiful, separation-afflicted night in exile that now I still wonder at it. For, several days later, I escaped in an extremely unexpected manner, on my own, not knowing Russian, across a distance that would have taken a year on foot. I was saved in a wonderful way through Divine favor, which came as a response to my neediness and impotence. Then, passing through Warsaw and Austria, I reached Istanbul. Being saved in this way, so easily, was quite extraordinary. I completed the long flight with an ease and facility that even a Russian-speaking, boldest and most cunning person might not have been able to accomplish.

That night in the mosque on the banks of the Volga made me decide: I will pass the rest of my life in caves. It is enough that I have long mixed in the social life of people. Since, finally, I will enter the grave alone, I will from now on choose solitude in order to become accustomed to loneliness.

But, regretfully, things of no use, like having many and important friends in Istanbul, and the glittering worldly life there, and in particular the fame and honor accorded to me which was far greater than my due, caused me to temporarily forget my decision. It was as though that night in exile was the iris and pupil of my life's eye, and the glittering white daytime of Istanbul, the lightless, white part of it, so that it could not foresee the future, and fell into sleep again. It was only two years later that *Ghawth al-Jilani* opened my eyes once more with his book *Futuhu'l-Ghayb* ("The Conquests Concerning the Unseen").

And so, elderly men and women! Know that the weakness and powerlessness of old age are means for attracting Divine grace and mercy. Just as I have observed this in myself on numerous occasions, the manifestation of mercy on the face of the earth demonstrates this truth clearly. For the most powerless and weakest of animals are the young. But it is also they who are favored with the sweetest and most beautiful manifestation of mercy. The powerlessness of a young bird in the nest at the top of a tree employs its mother like an obedient soldier as a manifestation of mercy. Its mother flies all around and brings it food. As soon as its wings grow strong and the nestling forgets its powerlessness, its mother says, "Go and search for your own food by yourself!" and no longer listens to it.

Just as this reality of mercy is in force for the very young, so too is it in force for the elderly, who are like the young in weakness and impotence. There have been many experiences that have given me the certain conviction that, in the same way that infants are sent their sustenance in a wonderful fashion by Divine Mercy because of their impotence, flowing forth from the springs of their mothers' breasts, so too the sustenance of the believing elderly, who have acquired innocence, is sent in the form of miraculous abundance. The part of a *hadith* which says,

> "Were it not for the elderly with their bent backs, calamities would descend on you in floods,"[10]

makes clear that a family's source of abundance is the elderly among it, and it is the elderly who preserve the family from the visitation of calamities.

---

[10] at-Tabarani, *al-Mu'jam al-Kabir*, 22:309; Abu Ya'la, *al-Musnad*, 11:287. (Tr.)

Since the weakness and powerlessness of old age are the means of attracting Divine mercy to this extent; since the wise Qur'an through the verses

> *Should one of them, or both, attain old age in your lifetime, do not say 'Ugh!' to them (as an indication of complaint or impatience), nor push them away; and always address them in gracious words. Lower to them the wing of humility out of mercy, and say: "My Lord, have mercy on them even as they cared for me in childhood".*

—Al-Isrā', 17:23-24

calls children, in the most wonderfully eloquent fashion, in five ways to be kind and respectful towards their elderly parents; since the Religion of Islam orders respect and compassion towards the elderly; and since human nature also requires respect and compassion towards the elderly; we elderly people certainly enjoy, in place of the temporary physical pleasures roused by appetites of youth, substantial, continual mercy and respect from Divine Grace and innate human feelings of tenderness, and the contentment of spirit that arises from such respect and compassion. This being the case, we should not wish to exchange this old age of ours for a hundred youths. I can tell you certainly that if they were to give me ten years of the Old or Former Said's youth, I would not give in exchange one year of the New Said's old age. I am content with my old age, and you too should be content with yours.

❈ Tenth Hope

After returning from captivity in Russia heedlessness overcame me for a year or two in Istanbul. During the days when the political atmosphere drew my attention away from myself to the outside world, I was once sitting on a high spot in the Eyüp Sultan graveyard overlooking the Golden Horn. I had a look around the horizons of Istanbul. I was suddenly overcome by such a state of mind that it was as if my private world was dying with my spirit being withdrawn in certain respects. Wondering whether the inscriptions on the gravestones were giving me such illusions, I withdrew my gaze. I looked not at the distance, but at the graveyard itself. Then the following was imparted to my heart:

> "This graveyard around you contains Istanbul a hundred times over, for Istanbul has been emptied here a hundred times. You cannot be an exception who can be saved from the judgment of the All-Wise and Powerful One, Who has poured all the people of Istanbul into here. You too will go."

I left the graveyard and with that awesome experience entered a small cell in Eyüp Sultan Mosque where I had stayed many times before. I thought to myself: I am a guest in three respects: I am a guest in this small room, I am also a guest in Istanbul, and in this world. A guest has to consider the journey. In the same way that I will leave this room, so one day I will leave Istanbul, and yet another day I will leave this world.

Amidst these reflections, my heart was overwhelmed by a most pitiful, grievous sorrow. For I was not losing only one or two friends; I would be parted from thousands of friends whom I loved in Istanbul, and I would also part from Istanbul, which I loved dearly. And as I would be parted from hundreds of thousands of friends in this world, I would also be parted from the beautiful world that I loved and with which I was infatuated. Pondering this, I went up once more to the high spot in the graveyard. Having been to the movie theatre from time to time in order to reflect and take lessons, just as the movie shows the images of dead people as if they were alive, moving around, that moment, all the dead of Istanbul appeared to me as corpses walking around. I said to my imagination: Since some of those in the graveyard appear to be walking around like people shown to move on a movie screen, so you should see those who are bound to enter the graveyard in the future as though they have entered it—they too are corpses, walking around.

All of a sudden, through the light of the Qur'an and through the guidance of *Ghawth al-A'zam*, Shaykh al-Jilani, my sorrowful state changed into a joyful, happy one. It was like this:

In the face of that sorrowful state, the light coming from the Qur'an reminded me: You had a few officer friends while you were in exile in Kosturma in the northeast of Russia. You knew that those friends would one day go to Istanbul. If one of them had asked you, "Would you go to Istanbul, or would you stay here?" certainly, if you had any intelligence, you would have gladly chosen to go to Istanbul. For out of a thousand and one friends, nine hundred and ninety-nine were already in Istanbul. Only one or two remained there, and they too would go to Istanbul one day. Going to Istanbul would not be a sad departure or a sorrowful separation for you. Moreover, at last, you came here and were you not happy to do so? You were delivered from the long, dark nights and cold, stormy winters in that enemy country. You came to this beautiful Istanbul, which resembled Paradise on the earth.

In the same way, from your childhood to your present age, ninety-nine out of a hundred of those whom you love have migrated to the graveyard; this is terrifying for you. You have only a few friends who are still in this world, and they too will go there.

Your death in this world is not separation; it is a reunion—a reunion with all those friends. They—those everlastingly alive spirits—have left behind under the soil their worn-out dwellings, some travelling about the stars and some through the levels of the Intermediate Realm.

The Qur'an and belief demonstrate this truth so certainly and convincingly that unless one is entirely lacking in heart and spirit, or unless misguidance has suffocated one's heart, it must be believed as though seeing it. For, most certainly and self-evidently, the All-Munificent and All-Compassionate Maker, Who adorns this world with His uncountable varieties of favors and gifts and so demonstrates His Lordship in an all-munificent and caring manner, preserving even the least significant things like seeds, would not annihilate or waste humanity—the most perfect, most comprehensive, and most important and beloved among His creatures—by sending it into eternal extinction or never-ending separation from those they love. Rather, as proven in the Tenth and Twenty-Ninth Words, like the seeds a farmer scatters over the earth, the All-Compassionate Creator temporarily takes that beloved creature of His under the ground, which is a door of mercy, in order to produce shoots in another life.

And so, after receiving this reminder from the Qur'an, the graveyard became more lovable to me than Istanbul. Solitude and seclusion became more pleasurable to me than conversation and company with people. And I found a place of seclusion for myself in Sarıyer on the Bosphorus. There, *Ghawth al-A'zam* al-Jilani, may God be pleased with him, became a master, doctor, and guide for me with his *Futuhu'l-Ghayb* ("Conquests Concerning the Unseen"), and Imam Rabbani, may God be pleased with him, a companion, a tender-hearted friend, and teacher with his

Mektubat ("The Letters"). Then I was extremely pleased I had entered upon old age, renounced the pleasures of modern civilization, and withdrawn from social life. I thanked God.

And so, respected people who have entered upon old age like me and frequently remember death through its warnings! In accordance with the light of the teachings of belief in the Qur'an, we should look favorably on old age, death, and illness, and even love them in one respect . Since we have an infinitely precious gift like belief, old age is agreeable, and illness and death likewise. If there are things that are disagreeable, they are sins, dissipation, heresy, unacceptable innovations in the Religion, and misguidance.

✸ Eleventh Hope

*A*fter my return from captivity, I was living together with my nephew Abdurrahman in a villa on the hill of Çamlıca in Istanbul. In respect of worldly life, my situation could have been thought to be the happiest for people like us: I had been saved from captivity, and in the *Darul-Hikmet al-Islamiya*[11] ("The House of Islamic Wisdom"), we were enjoying success in teaching and serving knowledge to the highest degree suited to my profession of teaching. The honor and attention afforded me was far greater than my due. I was living in Çamlıca, the most beautiful place of residence in Istanbul. Everything was perfect for me. I was together with my late nephew Abdurrahman, who was

---

[11] *Darul-Hikmet al-Islamiya* ("The House of Islamic Wisdom"), which was established in August 1918, was an Islamic academy. It was established in order to answer the questions posed to Islam, clarify the doubts raised concerning its precepts, and publish books to teach it. Bediüzzaman Said Nursi was one of its leading members. (Tr.)

extremely intelligent and self-sacrificing, and was both my student, and servant, and scribe, and who was like a son to me. While in this situation knowing myself to be more fortunate than anyone else in the world, one day I looked in the mirror and I saw grey hairs in my hair and beard.

Suddenly, the spiritual awakening I had experienced in the mosque in Kosturma while in captivity began again. As a result, I began reflecting upon the circumstances and causes to which I was inwardly attached and which I supposed to be the means of happiness in the life of the world. Whichever of them I thought about, I now saw it as rotten, unworthy of attachment, a delusion of sorts. In the meantime, I suffered an unexpected and unimaginable act of treachery and betrayal at the hands of a friend I had supposed to be most loyal. I felt frightened of the world. I said to my heart, "Have I been utterly deluded? I see that many people look with envy at our situation, which in reality should be pitied. Are all these people crazy, or am I now going crazy so that I see all these world-adoring people as such?"

Anyway, as a result of that intense awakening brought on by old age, first of all I took note of the transience of the short-lived things to which I felt attached. Then I took note of myself, and saw myself to be utterly powerless. Thereupon my spirit, which desired eternity and yet was deeply attached to transient things, supposing them to be eternal, pronounced most emphatically, "Since I am mortal regarding my body, what good can come from these mortal things? Since I am powerless, what can I expect from these powerless things? What I need is an All-Powerful, Everlasting One Who will provide a remedy for my ills." And I began to search.

Then, before all else, I had recourse to the learning I had been studying for so long, and searched for a consolation, a hope. Unfortunately, up to that time I had filled my mind with "natural" sciences and the sciences of philosophy as well as Islamic ones, and had mistakenly imagined those philosophical and "natural" sciences to be the source of personal development and means of enlightenment. However, those philosophical issues had greatly muddied my spirit and hindered my spiritual development. Suddenly, thanks to the Mercy and Grace of God Almighty, the sacred wisdom contained in the wise Qur'an came to my aid. As explained in several parts of the *Risale-i Nur*, it washed away and cleansed the dirt of those philosophical issues.

For instance, the spiritual veils of darkness coming from "natural" sciences had caused the outer world to suffocate my spirit. In whichever direction I turned to seek enlightenment, I could find not a beam of light in those matters, nor could I breathe. And so it continued until the extraordinarily brilliant light of Divine Unity taught by the Qur'an with the declaration, "There is no deity but God," dispersed all those veils of darkness, and I breathed easily. But based on what they had learnt from the people of misguidance and philosophers, my carnal soul and Satan attacked my reason and my heart. Thanks be to God, the ensuing debate with my soul resulted in the victory of my heart. Those exchanges have been narrated in part in several parts of the *Risale-i Nur*. Without needing to go further, in order to show one thousandth part of that victory of the heart, I will explain here only one proof out of thousands. I hope that it may also purify, to a certain extent, the spirits of certain elderly people who have dirtied their spirits in their youth and caused their hearts to be diseased, spoiling their souls with matters that are in part misguidance and in part trivialities—the matters taught or studied in the name of what they call modern philosophy or certain modern sciences. And may their spirits be saved from the evil that Satan and the carnal, evil-commanding soul provoke concerning Divine Unity.

The one proof out of a thousand is as follows:

My carnal, evil-commanding soul said in the name of science and philosophy, "Due to their very nature, things have a share in the existence and operation of the universe. Everything depends on a cause. The fruit has to be demanded from the tree and seed from the soil. So what does it mean to seek the tiniest and least insignificant thing from God and to entreat Him for it?"

Through the light of the Qur'an, the meaning and mystery of Divine Unity then unfolded and my heart said to my soul as follows:

The tiniest and least significant thing, just like the greatest and largest, issues directly from the Power of the Creator of the entire universe and emerges from His treasury. It cannot occur in any other way. Causes are merely a veil. For, in respect of art and creation, sometimes the creatures we suppose to be the tiniest and least significant are greater than the largest ones. Even if a fly is not greater than a chicken in art, it is not lesser than it. So, we should not make a difference between great and small. Either all should be attributed to material causes, or all should be ascribed at once to a single Being. And just as the former alternative is inconceivable, the latter is necessary and inevitably acceptable.

For if things and beings are attributed to a single Being, that is, to One Who is Eternal and All-Powerful, since His Knowledge—the existence of which the order of the universe and uncountable instances of wisdom in it establish and demonstrate with utter certainty—encompasses everything;

and since all things are determined in His Knowledge, each with a certain, particular measure; and since, manifestly, things and beings, infinitely full of art, constantly come into existence from nothing with infinite ease; and since, as has been convincingly demonstrated in many parts of the *Risale-i Nur* with numerous powerful proofs, the All-Knowing and All-Powerful One is absolutely able to create anything whatsoever with the command of *"Be!" and it is*, as simply as striking a match, He has limitless Power—this being so, the extraordinary ease and facility we observe in things coming into existence are due to the all-encompassing nature of that Knowledge and the limitless immensity of that Power.

For example, if the appropriate chemical solution is applied to a book written in invisible ink, that book suddenly reveals its existence and makes itself read. Just so, the particular form and nature of everything are determined in the all-encompassing Knowledge of that Eternal, All-Powerful One with a certain, particular measure. Like the chemical solution applied to invisible writing, through His limitless Power and penetrating Will, the Absolutely All-Powerful One applies with the command of *"Be!" and it is* a manifestation of His Power to the being which exists as knowledge, giving it external existence with utter ease and facility. He makes read the embroideries of His Wisdom.

If all things are not all at once attributed to that Eternal, All-Powerful One, the Knower of all things, then as well as having to assemble, for example, the body of the tiniest thing like a fly from the great variety of beings in the world, in a precise measure, the particles operative in that tiny fly's body will also have to know the mysteries of the fly's creation and its perfect art in all its minutest details. For, manifestly and as agreed by all intelligent people, natural or physical causes cannot create something from non- existence. If they were able to create, they would be assembling the body of even the tiniest being from most of the species of beings. And if they were to be assembling it, no matter which animate being, as there are within each being samples of most elements and most species, as each living creature is like a seed of the universe or an extract from it, they would necessarily have to obtain a seed from the entire tree or animate being from the entire earth, carefully putting them through a fine sieve and measuring them with the most sensitive balance. However, natural causes are ignorant and lifeless, and they have no knowledge that will allow them to determine a plan, a content, model, or program according to which they can melt and cast the particles to shape the exact form of any being without allowing dispersal or deformation. Moreover, there are infinite alternatives for a thing or being to take on a particular form; this requires that the lifeless and ignorant natural causes know which form they should give to each thing and thus gather and hold together, according to a certain, particular measure, the particles of the elements that flow like floods. So, anyone who does not suffer from blindness in their heart will see how distant from probability and reason is the idea that natural causes can create all these beings, each with an extraordinarily well-ordered body.

As a corollary of this truth, according to the meaning of the verse,

"Those whom, apart from God, you deify and invoke will never be able to create even a fly, even if all of them were to come together to do so."

—Al-Ḥajj, 22: 73

if all physical causes were to come together and if they had willpower, they could not assemble all the systems and organs of a single fly in the exact order and balance particular to it to form its body. Even if they were able to assemble them, they could not retain or preserve them in the specified measure required by the existence of that body. Even if they were able to retain or preserve them thus, they could not make the particles in that body, which are constantly renewed or replaced by new ones coming from the outside world, work in order. Therefore, self-evidently, physical causes cannot claim ownership of things, and their True Owner is someone else.

Indeed, their True Owner is One for Whom, according to theverse,

"Your creation and your resurrection are but as (the creation and resurrection) of a single soul."

—Luqmān, 31: 28

He revives all the living beings on the earth as easily as He revives a single fly. He creates the spring as easily as He creates a single flower, for He has no need to assemble things to create. Since He possesses the command *"Be!" and it is* and since every spring, in addition to the physical elements forming the bodies of beings, He also creates the innumerable attributes, states, and forms of innumerable beings from nothing, and since the plan, model, contents, and program of everything are already determined in His Knowledge, and since all particles and atoms move within the sphere of His Knowledge and Power, He creates everything with infinite ease, as though striking a match. And nothing confuses this motion in the least. In the same way that the planets are His obedient army, particles and atoms too move like a regular, well-ordered army for Him.

Since they move in dependence on that eternal Power, and operate in accordance with the principles of that eternal Knowledge, all things and beings come into existence with the invention of that Power. So, they should not be considered insignificant because they are small in body. Through the power it has because of its connection with that Power, a fly can destroy a Nimrod, an ant can ruin Pharaoh's palace, and the tiny seed of a pine caries the burden of a tree that is as tall as a mountain. We have proved this truth in numerous places in the *Risale-i Nur*. In the same way that due to his connection with the state as a member of the army, an ordinary soldier can take a king prisoner, thus far exceeding his own personal capacity, so too, due to their connection with the eternal Power, all things can be favored with and display miracles of art exceeding the capacity of their natural causes by hundreds of thousands of times.

In short, the fact that all things come into existence with both infinite art and infinite ease shows that they are the works of an Eternal All-Powerful One Who has all-encompassing Knowledge. Otherwise, because of hundreds of thousands of impossibilities, far from being possible, their existence would be absolutely unimaginable.

Through this most subtle, powerful, profound, and self-evident proof, my carnal, evil-commanding soul, which had been a temporary student of Satan and the spokesman for the people of misguidance and deviant philosophy, was silenced, and, all praise be to God, came to believe completely. It said:

I need such a Creator and Lord that He should know the least and most secret occurrences to my heart and my most secret appeals. And, just as He should answer the most hidden needs of my spirit, He should also have the power to replace this mighty world with the Hereafter in order to give me eternal happiness, and to create the heavens as easily as a fly, and to place a particle in the pupil of my eye just as He fastens the sun as an eye in the face of the sky. For one who cannot create a fly cannot do anything in relation to the thoughts of my heart and cannot hear the appeals of my spirit. One who cannot create the heavens cannot give me eternal happiness. In that case, my Lord is He Who both corrects and purifies the occurrences to my heart, and, as He fills and empties the skies with clouds in an hour, He will replace this world with the Hereafter, make Paradise, and open its doors to me, telling me to enter.

So, my elderly brothers and sisters, who, misled by some unfortunate considerations as my soul was, having spent part of your lives on lightless materialist philosophy and scientism! Understand from the sacred decree of *There is no deity but He*, which is perpetually pronounced by the Qur'an, just how powerful and true, how unshakeable and impregnable, how unchanging and sacred a pillar of belief this is, and how it disperses all spiritual darkness and cures all spiritual wounds!

In any case, due to the grey hairs appearing in my hair and beard and the treachery of an old friend, I felt disgust at the pleasures of Istanbul's glittering and apparently pleasant worldly life. My soul searched for spiritual pleasures in place of the pleasures with which it had been infatuated. It desired a light, a solace, in this old age, which the heedless think to be cold, burdensome, and unpleasant. And all praise be to God and countless thanks, just as I found the true, lasting, and sweet pleasures of belief in *There is no deity but He* and in the light of Divine Unity in place of all those false, unpleasant, fleeting and fruitless worldly pleasures, so too through the light of Divine

Unity, I saw old age (which the heedless think cold and burdensome) to be most light, and warm, and luminous.

And so, elderly men and women! Since you have belief and since you regularly pray and offer supplications which illuminate and strengthen belief, you can view your old age as eternal youth. For you can gain eternal youth through it. The old age that is truly cold, burdensome, ugly, dark, and full of pain is the old age of the people of misguidance; indeed, their youth is thus as well. They should weep and utter sighs and regrets. But you, respected believing elderly people should thank God and rejoice, saying,

"All praise and thanks be to God for every state!"

❖ Twelfth Hope

I was once being held in the district of Barla in the province of Isparta in distressing captivity under the guise of exile. I was in an extremely wretched state, suffering both illness and old age, and continuous separation from home, and in a village alone with no one, banned from all company and communication. Then, out of His perfect Mercy, God Almighty bestowed a light on me regarding the subtle points and mysteries of the wise Qur'an, which was a means of consolation for me. With it, I tried to forget my pitiful, grievous, sorrowful state.

I was able to forget my native land, my friends and relatives, but alas, there was one person I could not forget. That was Abdurrahman, who was both my nephew, although more like a son to me, and my most self-sacrificing student and most courageous friend. He had parted from me six or seven years before. He did not know where I was and thus he could not hasten to help or console me, nor did I know his situation so that I could correspond with him and confide in him. In that old age of mine, I was in need of someone faithful and self-sacrificing like him.

Then all unexpectedly, someone gave me a letter. I opened it and saw it was from Abdurrahman; it was a letter that showed his true nature. Exhibiting three manifest instances of wonder-working, part of which has been included in the Twenty-Seventh Letter.[12] It made me weep much; indeed, it still makes me weep. In the letter, the late Abdurrahman wrote earnestly and sincerely that he hated the pleasures of the world and that his greatest desire was to reach me and serve me in my old age just as I had taken care of him when he was a child. He also desired to help me with his powerful pen in publicizing the truths of the Qur'an, my true duty in this world. He even wrote, "Send me twenty or thirty treatises and I'll transcribe twenty or thirty copies of each and get others to transcribe them."

His letter afforded me great hope in respect of my affairs. Thinking that I had found a daring student with the intelligence of a genius, one who would serve me more faithfully and closely than a real (biological) son, I forgot my painful captivity, loneliness, separation from home, and old age.

Before writing that letter, he had a copy of the Tenth Word, which is about belief in the Hereafter. It was as if the treatise had been a remedy for him, curing all the spiritual wounds he had received during those six or seven years. He then wrote the letter to me as if he were anticipating his death with a truly strong and

---

[12] This contains the communications between Said Nursi and the students of the *Risale-i Nur* and which was published as separate books under the names of *Barla Lahikası* ("Supplements of Barla"), *Kastamonu Lahikası* ("Supplements of Kastamonu"), and *Emirdağ Lahikası* ("Supplements of Emirdağ"). (Tr.)

radiant belief. While I was once again thinking of spending a happy life with Abdurrahman, one or two months later I suddenly received news of his death. I was so shaken that five years later I am still under its effect. It caused a great sense of separation, grief, and sorrow, ten times exceeding that of the painful captivity, loneliness, separation, old age, and illness I was then suffering. I considered that half of my private world had died with the death of my mother, and now with Abdurrahman's death, I felt that the other half died. My ties with the world were now completely severed. For if he had lived, he could have been both a powerful help in my duties that pertain to the Hereafter, and a worthy successor to fill my place after me, as well as a self-sacrificing friend and a means of consolation in this world. He would have been my most intelligent student and companion, and a most trustworthy patron and protector of the *Risale-i Nur*.

From the viewpoint of being human, such losses are extremely painful and ravaging for people like me. It is true that, outwardly, I was trying to tolerate it, but in my spirit a fierce storm was raging. If from time to time the solace that came from the Qur'an's light had not been able to provide consolation for me, I would not have been able to bear it. At that time I used to go out alone to wander in the mountains and valleys of Barla. I sat in lonely places and, while surrounded by sorrows, pictures of the happy life I had spent in the past with my faithful students like Abdurrahman passed through my imagination like film scenes, and the grief caused by old age and exile broke my resistance. Suddenly, the meaning of the sacred verse,

Everything is perishable (and so perishing) except His "Face"
(His eternal Self, and what is done in seeking His good

pleasure). His alone is judgment and authority, and to Him you are being brought back.

—Al-Qaṣaṣ, 28: 88

was unfolded to me. It made me utter, "O Everlasting One, You are the Everlasting! O Everlasting One, You are the Everlasting!" and gave me true consolation.

Then, as described in the treatise, the Stairway of the *Sunnah* (the Eleventh Gleam), while in that sorrowful state in that desolate valley, inspired by this sacred verse, I saw myself at the head of three vast corpses:

I saw myself as a gravestone at the grave of the fifty-five dead Saids who were buried during the fifty-five years of my life.

The second corpse was the vast corpse of all my fellow human beings who had died since the time of Adam, peace be upon him, and who had been buried in the grave of the past. I saw myself as a tiny living creature like an ant moving on the face of this century, which is like the headstone of that grave.

The third corpse was the whole world which, as announced in the verse above, will one day die like human beings and the worlds that travel through it every year. This was embodied in my imagination.

Then the verse,

Still, if they turn away from you, say: "God is sufficient for me; there is no deity but He. In Him have I put my trust, and He is the Lord of the Supreme Throne".

—Al-Tawbah, 9: 129

came to my aid and with its true solace and inextinguishable light, it utterly removed that terrifying vision which arose from my sorrow at Abdurrahman's death. It reminded me: Since God Almighty exists, He is sufficient in place of everything else. Since He is Everlasting, He is surely sufficient. A single instance of His Grace substitutes for the whole world. And one manifestation of His Light gives life to the three vast corpses mentioned above, showing that they are not corpses, but rather they have completed their duties and have left for other worlds. As this truth has been explained in the Third Gleam, here I will only say that the two repetitions of the phrase, "O Everlasting One, You are the Everlasting! O Everlasting One, You are the Everlasting!" which indicates the meaning of *Everything is perishable (and so perishing) save His "Face"* (to the end of the verse), saved me from that most painful, sorrowful state. It was as follows:

The first time I uttered "O Everlasting One, You are the Everlasting!", like a surgical operation it began to cure the endless spiritual wounds caused by the passing of the world and the numerous friends to whom I was attached in this world, and by the severance of my bonds with them.

The second utterance of the phrase "O Everlasting One, You are the Everlasting!" was both an ointment and medication for all those innumerable wounds. It gave me the thought:

"You are everlasting. Let those who depart do so; You are sufficient for me. Since You are everlasting, one manifestation of Your Mercy is sufficient in the place of all things which are decaying. Since You exist, for one who is aware of one's connection with You through belief in Your Existence, and who acts in accordance with that connection in adherence to Islam, everything exists. Transience and decay, and death and departure are a veil, a renewal; they are like traveling through different realms."

Thinking this, my burning, exile-stricken, sad, painful, dark, and terrifying mood changed into a happy, joyful, pleasurable, luminous, lovable, companionable state. My tongue and heart—indeed, through the tongue of their disposition, each particle of my being—exclaimed, "All praise be to God!"

One thousandth of that manifestation of mercy is this: I returned to Barla from that valley where I suffered sorrows and where I was in a melancholy state of mind. I saw that a young man called Kuleönlü Mustafa had come to ask me a few questions concerning the five daily Prayers and ablutions. Although I was not accepting visitors at that time, as if through a presentiment my spirit perceived his sincerity of spirit and the future valuable services he would perform for the *Risale-i Nur*,[13] I did not turn him away and accepted him.[14] It later became clear that God Almighty had sent me Mustafa as an example (of future students of the *Risale-i Nur*) in place of Abdurrahman as a worthy successor who would completely fulfill·the duty of a true heir in the work of the *Risale-i Nur*, as though saying, "I took one Abdurrahman from you, but in return I will give you thirty Abdurrahmans like the Mustafa you see, who will be both students, and nephews, and son like companions, and brothers, and self-sacrificing friends in this duty for the Religion."

---

[13] By transcribing more than seven hundred copies of parts of the *Risale-i Nur* with his fine pen, Mustafa's younger brother, Küçük Ali, not only became an Abdurrahman but also trained many other Abdurrahmans.

[14] He truly demonstrated that he was not only worthy of being accepted, but also worthy of the future.

All praise be to God, He gave me thirty Abdurrahmans. So I told myself,

> "O weeping heart! Since you have seen this example and through it He has healed the most grave of your spiritual wounds, you should be convinced that He will heal all the rest of the wounds that afflict you."

And so, my elderly brothers and sisters who, like me, have lost a child or relative they love much during their old age, and who have to bear the intense sorrows of separation together with the burdens of old age! You have understood that while I was in a much more severe situation than yours, a single verse of the Qur'an healed it. So, in the sacred pharmacy of the wise Qur'an, there must certainly be remedies to heal all your afflictions. If you have recourse to it through belief and apply those remedies through regular worship, the heavy burdens of your old age and your sorrows will be greatly lightened.

The reason why this peace has been written relatively longer is to seek more prayers for Abdurrahman; let it not weary you. Also, what I pursue in showing my most painful and sordid wound in an extremely grievous and unpleasant way is to demonstrate what an extraordinary remedy and brilliant light is the sacred antidote of the wise Qur'an.

Thirteenth Hope

Here I will recount an important scene from the course of my life. It has to be somewhat lengthy, but I hope it will not become boring or tax your patience.

After being saved from captivity in Russia during the First World War, service to the Religion in the *Darul-Hikmet* kept me in Istanbul for two or three years. Then, through the guidance of the wise Qur'an and the spiritual assistance and influence of *Ghawth al-A'zam* al-Jilani and the awakening of old age, I felt wearied by the civilized life of Istanbul and troubled by its busy social scene. A longing for my native land drove me there. Thinking, since I am bound to die, let me die in my native land, I went to Van.[15]

I went first to visit my *medrese* in Van, the Horhor. I saw that the Armenians had burned it down during the Russian occupation, like all the other buildings of Van. It was adjacent to Van's famous fort, which is a huge, mountain-like monolith. My true friends, brothers, and close students of the *medrese*, which I had left seven or eight years before, were embodied before my eyes. Some of those self-sacrificing friends of mine had truly become martyrs, while others had died due to that calamity and become martyrs by default.

I could not help weeping. I climbed to the top of the fort, which overlooks the *medrese*, towering above it to the height of two minarets. I sat down there. I went back in memory seven or eight years. Having a powerful imagination, I wandered all around that time in my mind. Being alone, there was no one around to distract me from these imaginings or draw me back from that time. I saw enough changes over seven or eight years to fill a century.

I saw that the parts of the town at the foot of the fort and surrounding my *medrese* had been completely burnt and destroyed. Seeing this filled me with such sadness; it was as if two

---

[15] Van is a province of Turkey in Eastern Anatolia, bordering western Iran. (Tr.)

hundred years had passed between then and the time I had seen it before. Most of the people living in those houses had been my friends and acquaintances. The majority of them had died in the migrations, may God have mercy on them; they had become wretched in exile. Apart from the Armenian quarter, all the Muslim houses of Van had been demolished. My heartfelt a very sharp pain. I was so sorrowful that if I had had thousands of eyes, they would all have wept together. I had returned to my homeland from exile and supposed that I had been saved from exile. But alas! The most woeful exile I suffered was in my homeland. I saw that hundreds of my students and friends, with whom I had been connected in spirit, like Abdurrahman, who is mentioned in the Twelfth Hope above, had entered the grave and their places were all in ruins.

There was a saying that had long been in my mind, but which I had not been able to understand completely. Now in the face of that sorrowful scene I understood it completely. The saying was this:

"If there were to be no separation from friends, death could find no way to our souls enabling it to take them."[16]

That is to say, what causes humans to die most is separation from friends. Nothing had caused me as much suffering or sorrow as that situation. If help had not come from the Qur'an and belief, my grief and suffering would have almost made my spirit fly away.

Since early times, in their verses poets have lamented the destruction wreaked by time on the places where they were

---

[16] This saying is from Abu Tayyib al-Mutanabbi (for whom see footnote 59 at the end of the Eleventh Gleam): al-Hamawi, *Hizanat al-Adab*, 1:136. (Tr.)

together with their beloveds. Now I witnessed this with my own eyes in the most painful form. With the sorrow of one passing by the residences of beloved friends after two hundred years, my heart and spirit joined my eyes, and they all wept together. Then, one by one, the pleasing scenes of the life I had spent for nearly twenty years working with my dear students, when the places now lying in ruins before my eyes had been prosperous, joyful, and happy, came to life before me like pictures at the movies, then died away and vanished. These embodied scenes continued to pass before my eyes for some time.

Then I felt greatly astonished at worldly people: how can they deceive themselves? For the scene mentioned showed clearly that the world is transitory and that human beings are guests in it. I saw with my own eyes how true the continuously repeated words of the people of truth are: "The world is cruel, treacherous, evil; do not be deceived by it!" I also saw that just as humans are connected to their own bodies and households, so too are they connected with their town, their country, indeed with the whole world. For while weeping with just two eyes out of sorrow for the old age of my own being, I wanted to weep with ten eyes not only at the old age of my *medrese*, but also at its death. And I felt the need to weep with a hundred eyes at the half-death of my beautiful homeland.

There is a *hadith* that every morning an angel calls out,

"You are born to die, and
construct buildings to be destroyed."[17]

---

[17] al-Bayhaqi, *Shu'ab al-Iman*, 7:396; ad-Daylami, *al-Musnad*, 4:51. (Tr.)

I was not just hearing this truth with my ears now, but also seeing it with my eyes.

Ten years later when I recall that situation of mine, I still weep in the same way that it caused me to weep at that time. The houses at the foot of the old citadel, which had been standing there for thousands of years, were all in ruins, the town had aged eight hundred years within eight years, and my *medrese*, which had been quite prosperous and had acted as the gathering place of friends, had died with the great monolith of Van's fort becoming a gravestone to it, indicating the spiritual grandeur of its corpse; this was a sign of the death of all the *medrese*s in the Ottoman State.[18] It was as if my students, who had been together with me in the *medrese* eight years before, were weeping in their graves together with me. Indeed, the ruined walls of the town and its scattered stones were weeping with me. I saw them weeping.

Then I understood that I could not bear that exile in my homeland. I thought that I would either have to join them in the grave, or retreat into a cave in the mountains and await my death there. I told myself,

> "Since there are unbearable, burning separations which break patience and resistance in the world, surely death is preferable to life. Such a severe aspect of life cannot be endured."

I then cast my eyes in the six directions and saw them all to be dark. The unawareness of truth that arose from my intense grief showed me the world as a terrifying, void, desolate place that was about to collapse over my head. My spirit sought a point of

---

[18] All the *medrese*s were banned and abolished in the early years of the Republican Era in Turkey. (Tr.)

support in the face of uncountable hostile calamities, and a source of help to satisfy its endless desires extending as far as eternity, and awaited consolation in the face of the sorrow and grief that arose from endless instances of separation, devastation, and death. All at once, the reality expressed by the following verse of the Qur'an of miraculous exposition manifested itself:

Whatever is in the heavens and the earth glorifies God; and He is the All-Glorious with irresistible might, the All-Wise. To Him belongs the sovereignty of the heavens and the earth. He gives life and causes to die. He has full power over everything.

—Al-Ḥadīd, 57:1-2

It saved me from that pitiful, separation-stricken, terrible, sad imagining and opened my eyes. I saw that the fruits at the tops of the fruit-bearing trees were looking upon me with a smile. "Note us as well; do not look only at the ruins!" they were saying. The truth expressed by the verses brought the following thought to mind:

Why does a letter in the form of a town, which was inscribed by the hands of people who were guests on the page of Van's plain, and finally fell and was wiped out in a disastrous torrent called the Russian invasion, sadden you to this extent? Instead, consider the Eternal Inscriber, the True Owner and Master of everything, and see how His missives on this page of Van continue to be written in the same splendid fashion as you used to see. Your weeping because these places have become desolate ruins arises from the error of forgetting their True Owner, from not thinking that people are guests, and from imagining them to be in lasting possession.

A door to the truth opened up from that error and that burning scene, and my soul was prepared to accept it completely. Just as iron is put in the fire so that it becomes pliable and may be given a useful form, it was in the same way that that sorrowful state and terrible situation functioned as the fire that shaped my soul. Through the truth of the above verses, the Qur'an of miraculous exposition showed to my soul the radiation of the truths of belief, causing it to accept them.

All praise and thanks be to God, as is convincingly demonstrated in parts of the *Risale-i Nur* like the Twentieth Letter, through the radiation of belief, the truth expressed by the verses mentioned gave such a point of support to the spirit and heart—a support which can be developed in proportion to everyone's strength of belief—that it equipped me with the power to be able to resist calamities a hundred times more dreadful than the situation I then experienced. It reminded me: Everything is subjected to the command of the True Owner of this country, Who is your Creator. The reins of all things are in His hands. Your connection with Him is sufficient.

When I came to recognize my Creator and rely on Him, all the things that had appeared hostile no longer were so; and the sorrowful situations that had made me weep started to give me happiness. As we have demonstrated with sure proofs in many parts of the *Risale-i Nur*, the light issuing from belief in the Hereafter afforded such a source of help against my countless desires that it was sufficient not only for my attachment to my friends and connection with them in this insignificant, transient, and brief, worldly life, but also for my innumerable far-reaching desires in the world of permanence and eternal happiness. For through one manifestation of His Mercy, the All-Merciful and

All-Compassionate One every spring lays on the table of that season innumerable delightful, artful bounties on the face of this earth, which is His temporary guesthouse and one of the mansions in the universe, in order to please His guests for one or two hours. Then, after presenting these to them as an appetizer, He fills eight eternal Paradises with innumerable varieties for the eternal life of His servants. So, those who rely on the Mercy of such an All-Merciful and Compassionate One through belief and are aware of their relation with Him certainly find such a source of help that even its least degree provides for innumerable ambitions that extend as far as eternity, enabling their realization.

Furthermore, through the truth expressed in the above-mentioned verses, the light issuing from the radiation of belief showed itself so brightly that it lit up the six dark directions like daytime. It removed my sorrow that arose from the death of my students and friends and the destruction of my *medrese*, reminding me,

> "The world where your friends have gone is not dark. They have merely changed locations; you will meet with them again."

It brought an end to my tears and made me understand that I would find others who resembled them and who would take their place in this world.

All praise and thanks be to God, with the *medrese* of Isparta He raised to life the dead *medrese* of Van, and, in one sense, He raised my friends there to life with the more numerous and valued students and friends here. So I came to know that the world is not void or meaningless, and that my thinking of it in the form of a ruined wasteland had been wrong. Rather, as required by the

Wisdom of the True Master, the world changes its scenes that are made by people and renews His missives. Like the new fruit of a tree taking the place of those that have been harvested, death and separation in humankind are in fact renewal and refreshment. From the perspective of belief, they are a renewal which should not cause painful sorrow due to the want of friends, but a sweet sorrow that arises from parting in order to meet again in another, better place.

The verses also illuminated the face of the beings in the universe which had appeared dark because of the former appalling situation. Therefore, I wanted to offer thanks for this, and the following lines occurred to me in Arabic; they described that very reality. I said:

> All praise be to God for the light of belief, which shows that those who were thought to be strangers, antagonistic, lifeless, terrifying, and weeping orphans, in fact are lovable ones, brothers and sisters, living companions, employed for meaningful results, joyful, glorifiers of God and reciters of His Names.

Since I have the right to think of all the beings in my personal world, as well as in the entire world, as engaged in the praise and glorification of God, and through the intention to make use of them in these duties, together with all those beings, who praise and glorify God individually and collectively through the tongue of their disposition, I say, "All praise and thanks be to God for the light of belief."

Moreover, the true pleasures of life, which had been reduced to nothing because of my former heedless and appalling state of mind, and my hopes which had withered up entirely, and the bounties bestowed on me, which had been constricted, as has been explained in many other parts of the *Risale-i Nur,* so expanded that narrow sphere around my heart all at once through the light of belief that it contained the whole universe. In place of the bounties which had withered up in the garden of the Horhor *Medrese* and which had lost their taste, they made this world and the Hereafter each a merciful table of bounties. The light of belief showed not the ten or so human members like the eyes, ears, or the heart, but rather each of the hundred members in the form of such an extremely long arm which believers might stretch out each according to their degree that they could gather the bounties from all sides of those two tables of the All-Merciful. Therefore, in order to express this elevated truth and to give thanks for these limitless bounties, I uttered the following words:

> All praise and thanks be to my Creator for the bounty of the light of belief, for it shows the two realms of the world and the Hereafter as being full of bounties and mercy, from which every believer can rightfully benefit with their numerous senses able to develop by the leave of their Creator.

Since belief has so great an effect in this world, in the Realm of Eternity it will certainly have such fruit and radiation that they cannot be comprehended or described by the mind in this world.

And so, you elderly people who, like me, suffer the pains of separation from numerous friends because of old age! However much older than me in years the oldest of you is, in effect, I must be older than he. For since I feel extreme pity for my fellow beings due to the excessive compassion ingrained in my nature, and, because of that very compassion, I have suffered the pains of thousands of my brothers in addition to my own, I feel as though I have lived for hundreds of years. In addition, however much you may have suffered from the disaster of separation, you cannot have been exposed to that disaster to the degree that I have. For I have no child that I should think only of him or her. My deep innate feeling of pity and compassion causes me to feel pain and sympathy in the face of the sorrows of thousands of children, and even innocent animals. Neither do I have a house of my own that I should care for it only. Rather, being a Muslim, I am deeply bound to this country, and, in fact, the whole Muslim world, as though each were my own house. I feel great pain at the suffering of my fellow Muslims in these two great houses, and I am sorrowful at being separated from them.

And so, in the face of all these sorrows of mine that result from old age and the calamity of separation, the light of belief was enough for me; it gave me an inextinguishable hope and light and unending solace. So, it must certainly be more than enough for you in the face of the darkness, heedlessness, sorrow, and pains brought on by old age. In reality, the old age that is utterly dark and bereft of light and solace, and the most painful and terrible separation, is the old age and separation of the people of misguidance and the dissipated. In order to experience the belief which gives such hope, light, and solace, and its effects, one should be in a consciously worshipful attitude that is worthy of old age and appropriate to Islam. We cannot experience this by trying to imitate the young, plunging our head into heedlessness, and forgetting old age.

Consider the *hadith*, the meaning of which is,

"The best of the young among you are those who resemble the old in care and avoidance of vice, while the worst of your elderly are those who imitate the young in vice and heedlessness."[19]

My elderly brothers and sisters! There is another *hadith* which says,

> "Divine Mercy is ashamed to leave unanswered the prayers offered to the Divine Court by an elderly believer of sixty or seventy years."[20]

Since Divine Mercy holds you in such respect , be respectful towards this respect by worshipping Him!

❈ Fourteenth Hope

The Fourth Ray, explaining the luminous Qur'anic statement,

"God is sufficient for us".

—Āl 'Imrān, 3:173

says in the beginning, in summary:

Due to the worldly people having isolated me from everything, I was suffering five sorts of separation. Without looking to the consoling and helpful lights of the *Risale-i Nur*, because of heedlessness arising from distress, I turned to my heart and spirit. I saw that together with an infinite impotence and boundless neediness, an extremely powerful love of permanence, an intense attachment to existence, and a great yearning for life were dominating me. But an awesome mortality was extinguishing that permanence. In that mood, I exclaimed like the

---

[19] at-Tabarani, *al-Mu'jam al-Kabir*, 22:83; Abu Ya'la, *al-Musnad*, 13:467. (Tr.)

[20] at-Tabarani, *al-Mu'jam al-Awsat*, 5:270. (Tr.)

poet who suffers separation:

> While my heart desired permanence, God, the Truth,
> judged the mortality of my body;
> I am afflicted with an incurable ill;
> how pitiful it is that Luqman is unaware of it!

I bowed my head in despair. Suddenly the verse,

"God is sufficient for us; how excellent a Guardian He is!"

—Āl 'Imrān, 3: 173

came to my aid, and asked me to read it attentively. So I recited it five hundred times every day. While reciting it, out of its numerous invaluable lights, nine aspects of God's sufficiency[21] were unfolded to me, not only at the level of "certainty coming from knowledge," but at that of "certainty coming from observation."

The first luminous aspect of God's sufficiency

My innate love of permanence, which essentially arises from a manifestation in my being of a Name of the One of Perfection and Majesty, Who is naturally loved because of His absolute Perfection, and which should therefore have been directed towards the Essence, Perfection, and Permanence of that Absolutely Perfect One, had lost its way and become attached to the shadow due to heedlessness. It had sought the permanence of the worldly life, which is nothing more than a transitory mirror of what is essentially eternal. Then the Qur'anic statement, *God is sufficient for us*, came and lifted up the veil. I observed and felt

---

[21] Six aspects of God's sufficiency are mentioned here. (Tr.)

and experienced with the degree of "absolute certainty" that the true pleasure and happiness of my permanence lay accurately and in more perfect form in the Permanence of the Everlasting One of Perfection and in believing and confirming that He is my Lord and Deity. The proofs for this have been explained in the Fourth Ray (included in *The Rays*), the treatise on the verse *God is sufficient for us*, in twelve consecutive paragraphs in a fine, profound way.

The second luminous aspect of God's sufficiency

At a time when old age, exile, solitude, and isolation were added to my endless impotence in nature, when "the worldly" were attacking me with their schemes and spies, I told my heart, "Armies are attacking a single man whose hands are tied, and who is ill and weak. Is there not a point of support for me?" I had recourse to the verse, *God is sufficient for us; how excellent a Guardian He is*, and it informed me of the following:

Through the document of belief you become connected to such a Ruler of Absolute Power that every spring He equips in perfect order all the armies of plants and animals on the earth, which is composed of hundreds of thousands of different nations. In addition, as the All-Merciful, He places in tiny protective cases the sustenance of all animals and humans in the form of the extracts of all kinds of foods, which we call seeds and grains and which may be likened to the meat, sugar and other food extracts discovered recently, but a hundred times more perfect than them. He includes in those extracts the instructions of Divine Destiny concerning their growth and development into edible foods. The creation of those tiny cases and their growth into elaborate tables of food take place with such speed, ease, and abundance in the factory of *Kâf-Nûn,* forming the command of "*Kun!* [Be!]," that the Qur'an states that the Creator merely commands and it comes into being.[22] Since you have such support through the connection to Him enabled by the document of belief, you can rely on an infinite strength and power. As I learned this lesson from the verse, I found such a moral strength that I felt I had enough power of belief to challenge not only my present enemies, but the entire world. With all my spirit I proclaimed,

"God is sufficient for us; how excellent a Guardian He is!"

The third luminous aspect of God's sufficiency

Having found my attachment to the world to have been severed after suffering the oppression of those exiles and illnesses, belief recalled to me that I was destined for perpetual happiness in an eternal world, an everlasting realm. I then gave up sighing regretfully, which only caused further grief and yearning, and became cheerful and happy. However, this ideal or goal of the spirit and the final result of human nature could only be realized through the infinite Power of an Absolutely All-Powerful One, Who knows and records the action and rest and conduct and states, in word and deed, of all His creatures, and through His conferring limitless favor and importance on humans, whom He takes as His friends and addressees, and to whom He has given a rank superior to all beings despite their absolute impotence. Reflecting on these two points—namely, the activity of such a Power and the importance in reality of apparently impotent and insignificant human beings—I sought an explanation that would deepen belief and satisfy the heart. Again I had recourse to the

---

[22] The writer refers to the verse, *When He wills a thing to be, He but says to it "Be!" and it is* (Yā Sīn, 36:82). (Tr.)

verse, *God is sufficient for us; how excellent a Guardian He is,* and it told me to note the suffix "*-na,*" ("for *us*") and to be attentive to the beings that are saying, "*God is sufficient for us,*" with me either verbally or through the tongue of their disposition.

I at once looked and saw that innumerable birds and flies (which are miniature birds) and innumerable animals, plants and trees were, like me, reciting, *God is sufficient for us; how excellent a Guardian He is!* through the tongue of their disposition. They recall to everyone the following fact: that they have such a Guardian Who guarantees all their essential necessities of life that before our eyes and particularly in the spring, His vast and All-Majestic Power creates in utmost abundance, with the greatest ease, on a vast scale, with the greatest art, and in balanced and well-ordered fashion, and in forms all different from one another, with no defect, fault, or confusion at all, from eggs, drops of fluids, grains, and seeds that look very much like each other and whose component elements are the same, a hundred thousand species of birds, hundreds of thousands of animals, hundreds of thousands of types of plants, and hundreds of thousands of varieties of trees. The similarity and resemblance among all these beings despite the infinite difference demonstrate to us His Unity and Oneness, and inform us that there cannot be any interference or participation in those acts of His Lordship and Creativity. Those who want to understand my personal identity and human nature as a believing man, which is like that of all believers, should look at the meaning of the 'I' included in the first person plural 'us' in *God is sufficient for us.* What is my apparently insignificant, needy being, or that of any believer? What is life? What is humanity? What is Islam? What is certain, verified belief? What is knowledge of God? How should love be? They can find the answers to all these questions.

The fourth luminous aspect of God's sufficiency

Once, when in an instance of heedlessness in which I felt overpowered by circumstances like old age, exile, illness, and defeat, I was painfully anxious about my being, to which I was intensely attached and with which I was infatuated. I was anxious that my being, as well as all other creatures, were heading for death, were being stripped of existence. So, once again, I had recourse to the verse. It said to me, "Note my meaning; look at it through the telescope of belief!"

So I looked with the eye of belief and saw that like all other believers, my minuscule being was the mirror of an Unlimited Being, and through infinite expansion, the means of gaining innumerable existences, and a word of wisdom yielding the fruits of numerous permanent existences more valuable than itself. So, I knew with the certainty of knowledge that to live in connection with that Being, even for an instant, was as valuable as eternal existence. For I understood through the consciousness of belief that my being was a work of art and a manifestation of the Necessarily Existent Being. So, being saved from the essentially groundless anxieties of loneliness and from innumerable separations and their pains, I formed relations and bonds of brotherhood with beings that I love, to the number of Divine acts and Names responsible for beings and especially living ones, and I knew that there was a permanent union with all of them after a temporary separation. And so, through belief and connection with the Creator and all of His creatures through belief, like all believers, my being gained the lights of innumerable existences untainted by separation. Even when my being departs, as they remain behind, it is as happy as if it too had remained.

In short, death is not separation, it is union; it is a change of location; it is producing an eternal fruit.

The fifth luminous aspect of God's sufficiency

At another time, my life was once more shaken by very harsh conditions, and drew my attention to itself. I saw that my life was going swiftly, drawing close to the Hereafter; it had started to be extinguished under harsh conditions. I thought sorrowfully that, as explained where the Divine Name, the All-Living is discussed in the *Risale-i Nur* with its important functions and great merits and benefits, life did not deserve to be so swiftly extinguished, but rather should endure a long time. I again had recourse to my teacher, the verse, *God is sufficient for us; how excellent a Guardian He is!* This time it said to me,

> "Consider life from the perspective of the All- Living and Self-Subsisting by Whom all subsist, Who gives you life!"

I did so and saw that if my life looks to me in one respect , it looks to the All-Living and the Self-Subsisting in a hundred. And if, out of its results, one looked to me, a thousand looked to my Creator. Therefore, one instant of its endurance within the bounds of God's good pleasure and approval is sufficient; a long time is not required. This truth has been explained in five indications and four matters in the Thirtieth Gleam in this book. Those who are not dead or who want to be alive should seek the nature and reality of life and its true rights in these indications and matters; they will find them and be raised to life!

A summary is as follows: the more life is grasped, causing it to look to the All-Living and the Self-Subsisting, and the more belief becomes the life and spirit of life, the more it becomes perpetual and yields enduring fruits. It also becomes so elevated that it receives the manifestation of eternity. It is no longer a consideration whether life is short or long.

The sixth luminous aspect of God's sufficiency

At a time when old age was reminding me of my personal departure from the world amidst the events of the end of time, which suggest the overall destruction of the world—the time of general parting, my innate love of beauty and fondness for perfection were being developed in an extraordinarily sensitive manner. With extraordinary awareness and sorrow I saw that transience and decline, which are always destructive, and death, which is the continuous cause of separation, were pounding this beautiful world and these lovely creatures in a terrible manner and destroying their beauty. When my innate love of creation boiled up intensely and rebelled against this situation, once more I had recourse to the verse *God is sufficient for us; how excellent a Guardian He is!* to find consolation. It said to me, "Recite me and consider my meaning carefully!"

So I entered the observatory of verse 35 of *Surat an-Nur, God is the Light of the heavens and the earth* (to the end of the verse), and looked through the telescope of belief to the most distant levels of the verse, *God is sufficient for us; how excellent a Guardian He is!* and through the microscope of the insight of belief at its most subtle meanings. I saw the following:

Mirrors, pieces of glass, transparent things, and even bubbles manifest the various hidden beauties of the sun's light and the seven colors in its light; and through their disappearance, renewal, and replacements with new ones and with different capacities and refractions, they cause the renewal and remanifestations of these beauties. In the same way, in order to act as mirrors to the sacred

Beauty of the All-Gracious, Beautiful One of Majesty, the Eternal Sun, and to the permanent beauties of His All-Beautiful Names, and to cause the ever-renewal of their manifestations, these beautiful creatures, these lovely beings arrive and depart in a constant flux. As explained in detail in the *Risale-i Nur* with powerful evidence, they demonstrate that the beauties manifested by them are not their own property, but the signs, indications, gleams, and manifestations of an eternal, transcendent, sacred Beauty Which wants to become manifest. Anyone with a sound mind and heart who reads them will understand and confirm that their existence, as well as the existence of everything, is a miracle, and they will try to develop it.

❊ Fifteenth Hope

When I was once in enforced residence in Emirdağ,[23] in what was virtually solitary confinement, I became wearied of life because of the torments inflicted on me through unbearable surveillance and pressure. I regretted having been released from prison and longed for Denizli Prison with all my spirit, even wishing to enter the grave. But, even as I was thinking that prison or the grave were preferable to a life like this, Divine Grace came to my aid and bestowed on me the students of the *Medresetu'z-Zehra* , whose pens were like the duplicating machines that had just been invented. All at once, five hundred copies of each of the valuable collections of the *Risale-i Nur* appeared; one pen had become five hundred. The fact that this work gained new hearts on a wider scale made me love that distressing life, causing me to offer endless thanks.

A while later, the covert enemies of the *Risale-i Nur* could no

---

[23] Emirdağ is a district of Afyon, a province in the west of Turkey. (Tr.)

longer bear its victories, and provoked the government against us. Again life started to become difficult for me. Then suddenly, Divine Grace showed itself: the officials connected with the case, who were in fact most in need of the *Risale-i Nur*, studied the confiscated copies of it in connection with their duties with great curiosity and care, and their hearts became friendly to it. When they began to appreciate this work instead of criticizing it, the *Risale-i Nur* circle of study greatly expanded. It produced spiritual profits a hundred times greater than our material losses, reducing our anxiety and distress to nothing.

Then, secret, hypocritical enemies drew the government's attention to my person. They recounted my political activities during my days of the Old or Former Said. They caused both the justice department, and the education authorities, and the police, and the Ministry of Internal Affairs to be suspicious of me. Due to certain political trends and the provocation of certain communists, who were in fact anarchists, the suspicions became more widespread. They started to pressure us and arrest us, and confiscate those parts of the *Risale-i Nur* that came into their hands. The activities of the *Risale-i Nur* students came to a standstill. With the thought of disgracing me in the sight of people, a number of officials made false accusations so absurd that no one could have believed them at all. They tried to spread the most incredible slander, but they could not make anyone believe it.

Then on some most trivial pretext they arrested me during the intensely cold days of winter, and kept me in solitary confinement in prison, in a large and extremely cold cell that had no form of heating. When in my small room I had been accustomed to light my stove several times a day, and had always had live coals in the brazier because of my weakness and illness. Despite this, I was only able to endure the cold with great difficulty because of my weakness and illness. While struggling in the cell, suffering both from fever caused by the cold and from a dreadful distress and anger, a truth unfolded in my heart through Divine Grace. What follows occurred to my spirit:

You called prison the *"Medrese-i Yusufiya"*—the School of the Prophet Joseph. And while in the Denizli prison, circumstances a thousand times greater than your distress caused such spiritual gain that other prisoners benefited from the *Risale-i Nur*, and its conquests were on a larger scale; this caused you to offer thousands of thanks instead of complaining. They made each hour of your imprisonment and hardship equal to ten hours of worship, and those transient hours became eternal. God willing, the fact that those who suffer imprisonment in your third School of Joseph will benefit from the *Risale-i Nur* and find consolation in it will warm this cold, severe hardship of yours and transform it into joy. If those with whom you are angry have been deceived, then they are ill-treating you unknowingly. So, they do not deserve anger. But if they are tormenting you and causing you suffering knowingly, out of spite and on account of misguidance, soon they will enter the solitary confinement of the grave through the eternal execution of death, where they will suffer incessant torment. On account of their oppression, you are both earning merit and spiritual pleasures, and making your transient hours eternal, and performing scholarly and religious duties with sincerity.

With all my strength I uttered, "All praise and thanks be to God!" Being a human, I pitied those tyrants and prayed, "O my Lord, reform them!" As I wrote in my statement to the Ministry of

Internal Affairs, those responsible for this new incident, which was completely unlawful in at least ten respects, were themselves the guilty ones. Those tyrants had acted unlawfully even in the eyes of human law. Through the most incredible pretexts they had contrived such slanders and fabrications that those who heard them laughed and lovers of truth wept, demonstrating to the fair-minded that they had been completely unable to find a way to attack the *Risale-i Nur* or its students according to the law or to justice, and therefore they had deviated into lunacy.

For instance, the officials who had spied on us for a month could find nothing to accuse us of, so they wrote a note that said, "Said's servant bought *raki* from a shop and took it to him." Unable to find anyone to sign the note, they finally picked up a drunken, uncivilized man and tried to bully him into signing it. Even he said, "God forgive us! Who would sign this most incredible lie?" So they were compelled to tear it up.

A second example: Someone I did not know personally and still do not know loaned me his horse so that I could take an excursion into the country. Because of my illness and in order to take some air, I would go out most days for a couple of hours in summer. Following my rule and in order not to feel indebted to anyone, I had promised the owner of the horse and the carriage (that came with it) books worth fifty *lira*. Is there any danger in such a thing? But as though it was an important political event or an incident that affected public security, the governor, the court officials, and the police asked us nearly fifty times who the horse belonged to. In order that this meaningless questioning might come to an end, out of human tenderness, one person said that the horse was his and another that the carriage was his. They were both arrested with me. We faced numerous childish games such as these and sometimes we laughed and sometimes we cried. We understood that those who attacked the *Risale-i Nur* and its students only made fools of themselves.

A peculiar conversation from among these incidents is as follows: On the paper authorizing my arrest it was recorded that it was for "disturbing public order." Without having seen the document, I told the public prosecutor, "I spoke behind your back last night. I said to a police officer who was questioning me on behalf the Chief of Police, 'If I have not served the public security of this country to the same degree as a thousand public prosecutors and a thousand police chiefs—I repeated this three times—may God damn me!'"

Then at that point, in those freezing conditions, I was almost overcome by anger and annoyance with those whose hatred and ill intentions had sent me into this unbearable exile, isolation, arrest, and oppression at a time when I was most in need of rest, of avoiding catching cold and being anxious about the world. Divine Grace came to my aid, and it occurred to my heart as follows:

Divine Destiny, which is pure justice, has a large part in the oppression which these people are inflicting on you. You have food to eat in this prison; that provision of yours called you here. You should respond with contentment and resignation. The Wisdom and Mercy of the Lord have also a significant part in this situation: you should try to enlighten those in this prison and console them, so you might gain reward. Your response should be thousands of thanks and great patience. Your soul also has a part in this situation because of certain faults you may be unaware of. Your response should be repentance and seeking forgiveness, telling your soul that it deserved this blow. Also, some of your secret enemies have a part in it, through their deceitful intrigues that provoke certain ingenuous and suspicious officials to such oppression. In response to this, the powerful immaterial blows dealt by the *Risale-i Nur* to those hypocritical ones have sought your revenge completely. That is enough for them. Finally, the officials who were the actual means of bringing about this situation have a part in it. Your response should be—so that they may benefit from the *Risale-i Nur* through belief, whether they want to or not, and even if they came to it with the intention of criticizing it—to forgive them according to the rule,

The God-revering, righteous ones—those who ... ever-restrain their rage (even when provoked and able to retaliate), and pardon people (their offenses).

—Āl 'Imrān, 3: 134

that would be an act of magnanimity.

Due to the perfect contentment and gratitude I felt as a result of this veritable warning, I decided to remain in this new "School of Joseph," and even to commit some harmless offence which would inflict upon me a prison sentence so that I might help even those who were opposed to me. Furthermore, I was seventy-five years old, without any worldly attachment, and out of seventy of those whom I loved only five remained alive. Besides, seventy thousand copies of the *Risale-i Nur* collection were in free circulation and would perform my duties, and in addition, I had brothers and sisters and heirs who would serve belief with thousands of tongues in place of my one tongue. Therefore, the grave was a hundred times better for me than this prison. And the prison was a hundred times more comfortable and more beneficial than liberty outside that had no freedom and which was subject to tyranny and oppression. For in place of having to suffer all alone outside the oppression of hundreds of officials, in prison, with hundreds of other prisoners, one only had to suffer the slight "formal" oppression of one or two people, like the prison governor and chief warder. But one receives the brotherly kindness and consolation of many companions in prison. In addition, Islamic compassion and human innate tenderness lead to the kind treatment of the elderly in such a position, thus turning the hardship of prison into mercy. In consideration of all these, I became resigned to prison.

When I went to court for this third trial, because of my difficulty in remaining standing due to weakness, old age, and illness, I sat on a chair outside the door of the trial room. The judge suddenly appeared and angrily asked in a spiteful manner, "Why isn't he waiting standing up?" I became angry at this mercilessness in the face of old age. Suddenly, I saw that a large number of Muslims had gathered around us and were watching with complete affection and brotherly compassion, and not dispersing. The following two truths occurred to me:

The first: The secret enemies of myself and the *Risale-i Nur* had deceived certain ingenuous officials in the hopes that in this way they could put a stop to the *Risale-i Nur*'s conquests by destroying the public's good opinion of me and damaging my reputation—something that in any case I did not want. They had provoked those officials to act disdainfully towards me in that way. But in place of that one man's insults, see these hundred people as a Divine favor for the *Risale-i Nur*'s service to belief! Appreciating your service, they pity you and are offering their sympathy, and they welcome you and see you off. Indeed, the next day while I was answering the public prosecutor's questions, about a thousand people gathered in the courtyard outside the court windows, showing their concern. It was as though they wished to tell the authorities not to oppress me. The police were unable to make them disperse. It occurred to me that in this perilous age these people desire true solace, an inextinguishable light, a powerful belief, and certain glad tidings about eternal happiness—by their very nature, they were searching for these. They must have heard that what they were searching for existed in the *Risale-i Nur*, and this was the reason why they showed my unimportant person such attention and regard for the little service I had performed for belief—the attention and regard that far exceeded my due.

The second truth: It occurred to me that in return for the insulting ill-treatment of a few deceived individuals which they inflicted on us due to their ungrounded suspicions that we were disturbing public order and with the intention to prevent our service for belief and to destroy public acclaim and regard for us, came the applause and appreciation of innumerable people of truth and forthcoming generations.

Through the strength of certain, verified belief, in every part of this country the *Risale-i Nur* and its students have halted the dreadful corrupting efforts of anarchy that shelter under the veil of communism and which are trying to destroy public order. The *Risale-i Nur* and its students work to maintain public order and security, and as a result in over twenty years three or four courts and the police in ten provinces have not been able to find or record any incidents of public order violation by the *Risale-i Nur* students, who are very numerous and found in every part of the country. And some fair-minded police officers in three provinces have stated, "The *Risale-i Nur* students are moral police. They help us with the preservation of public order. Through certain, verified belief, something is left in everyone's head who reads the *Risale-i Nur* that prevents them from committing any offense. They work to secure public order."

An example of this was Denizli prison. When the *Risale-i Nur,* including in particular *Meyve Risalesi* (The Treatise on the Fruits of Belief), which was written in that prison, entered there, within a period of three or four months the prisoners, numbering more than two hundred, became so extraordinarily obedient and acquired such religious, righteous conduct that a man who had killed three or four people held back from even killing bedbugs. They became completely compassionate, harmless and beneficial members of the nation. The officials observed this change in amazement and appreciation. Before receiving their sentences, some youths even said: "If the students of the *Risale-i Nur* remain in prison, we will try to have ourselves convicted so that we can be taught by them and become like them. We will reform ourselves through their teaching."

So, those who accuse the *Risale-i Nur* students, who are of that quality, of disturbing public order are surely seriously mistaken, or have been deceived, or knowingly or unknowingly are deceiving the government for the sake of anarchy, and trying to crush us through oppression. We say the following to them:

> Since death cannot be killed and the grave is not to be closed, and the travelers in this guesthouse of the world, convoy after convoy, enter the earth with great speed and ado, and disappear, certainly we too will part from one another very soon. You will receive the punishment for your oppression in a terrible fashion. You will mount the gallows of death, which

is a door to eternal punishment for you but the discharge papers for the oppressed people of belief. The passing pleasures you have received in this world, which you imagine to be permanent, will change into everlasting, grievous pain.

Regrettably, our covert hypocritical enemies sometimes attach the name of " Sufi order" to the truth of Islam, which has been gained and preserved with the efforts of hundreds of millions of martyrs of the rank of saints and heroic veterans of this religious nation. While the way of Sufi orders is only a single ray of the Sun of Islam, they attempt to show it as the sun itself, and deceive certain careless government officials. Labeling the *Risale-i Nur* students, who in fact work effectively for the truths of the Qur'an and belief, as "followers of a Sufi order" and "members of a political society," they wish to provoke such officials against us. We say to them, and to those who lend an ear to them against us, what we told the fair court at Denizli:

> Let us too be sacrificed for a sacred truth, for which hundreds of millions of others have been sacrificed! Even if you set fire to the world to burn us, we who sacrifice ourselves for the truths of the Qur'an will not lay down our "arms" before heresy; by God's will and help, we will not abandon our sacred duty!

And so, because of the sacred solace for the pains and despairing condition of my old age that emanates from belief and the Qur'an, I would not exchange even the most distressing year of my old age for ten of the happiest years of my youth. Particularly so, as every hour in prison of those who repent and perform the obligatory Prayers is equal to ten hours of worship under normal conditions, and each transient day spent in illness and oppression gains the reward of ten days of perpetual life, I have understood how deserving of thanks are these days for someone like me who is awaiting his turn at the door of the grave. I utter, "Endless thanks be to my Lord!" and am content with my old age and pleased with my imprisonment. For life does not cease; it passes swiftly. If it passes in pleasure and happiness, since the disappearance of pleasure is pain, it causes regret and grief, and due to thanklessness and heedlessness, it departs leaving sins in its wake. Whereas, if it passes in prison or hardship, since the disappearance of pain is a pleasure in spirit, and since it is considered to be a sort of worship, it becomes perpetual in one respect , and through its good fruits, gains permanence. It becomes atonement for the sins committed in the past and the mistakes that were the cause of imprisonment, purifying them. From this perspective, those among the prisoners who perform at least the compulsory parts of the obligatory Prayers should offer thanks in patience.

❈ Sixteenth Hope

Once in my old age I was released from the Eskişehir prison after serving a year's sentence. They exiled me to Kastamonu (in northern Turkey), where they kept me for two or three months as a guest in the police station. It may be understood how much distress someone like me suffered in a place like that; how difficult this was for one who prefers solitude, one who is wearied by meeting even loyal friends, and one who cannot endure the change of his classical, native dress. While in such tormenting conditions, Divine Grace suddenly came to the aid of my old age. The inspector and police officers in the police station became like faithful friends. They did not once warn me about how I dressed, and, as if they were my servants, they used to take me for trips around the town.

Then I took up residence in Kastamonu's *"Risale-i Nur Medrese,"* opposite the police station, and started to write more of the *Risale-i Nur*. Heroic *Risale-i Nur* students like Feyzi, Emin, Hilmi, Sadik, Nazif, and Salahaddin attended the *Medrese* in order to duplicate the treatises in their handwriting and distribute them. We held scholarly debates even more profound than those I had held in my youth with my former students.

Then our secret enemies aroused the suspicions of some officials and some egotistical *hoja*s and *shaykh*s concerning us. They caused us and the *Risale-i Nur* students from five or six provinces to be gathered together in the "School of Joseph" of Denizli prison. The details of this Sixteenth Hope are to be found in the short letters sent from Kastamonu and those I secretly sent to my brothers while in Denizli prison, and in the collection containing the court defense speeches. So referring the details to those letters and to my defense speech, I will cut it short here:

I hid certain confidential and important treatises under the coal and firewood so that they might be published after my death or after the top ranking authorities in the capital city listened to the truth and came to their senses. While I was feeling relaxed about this, some detectives and the assistant public prosecutor suddenly raided my house. They pulled out those confidential and important treatises from under the wood. Afterwards, they arrested me and sent me to Isparta prison, although I was in bad health. While I was greatly upset and extremely saddened at the harm that had come to the *Risale-i Nur*, Divine Grace came to our aid. The authorities began to read with great care and curiosity these important treatises which had been hidden, and of which they were much in need, and the government offices became like *Risale-i Nur* study centers. Having started to read with the intention of criticizing, they began to appreciate them. Even in Denizli, although we were unaware of it, numerous official and unofficial people read the secretly printed edition of *Ayetü'l-Kübra* (The Supreme Sign), and their belief was strengthened. This reduced to nothing the disaster of prison that we were suffering.

Later they took us to Denizli prison, and put me into solitary confinement in a stinking, cold, damp cell. While struggling with old age, illness, and the unhappiness that arose from the troubles my friends were suffering because of me, as well as the grief and distress caused by the confiscations of the parts of the *Risale-i Nur* and the cessation in its activities, Divine Grace suddenly came to my aid. It changed that huge prison into a *Risale-i Nur Medrese*, proving it to be a School of Joseph. The *Risale-i Nur* started to spread through the diamond pens of the heroes of the *Medresetu'z-Zehra*. In those severe conditions, one of those heroes, who is the most advanced in serving the *Risale-i Nur*, copied out more than twenty copies of the Fruits of Belief and the Collection of Defense Speeches in the space of three or four months. They began to conquer minds and hearts both within the prison and outside. This changed our losses in that disaster into great gains and our distress into joy. It once again demonstrated the truth in the verse,

"It may well be that you dislike a thing but it is good for you."

—Al-Baqarah, 2: 216

Then due to the harsh criticisms of the first Experts Committee, based on incorrect and superficial official reports, and due to the dreadful attacks by the Education Minister and the statement he published against us, as well as some press releases, things went so far that they even tried to have some of us executed. While in these circumstances, Divine Grace came to our aid. First of all, against all expectations, an appreciative report came from the Experts Committee in Ankara. In addition, we proved in court that certain points that they had shown to be errors in the *Risale-i Nur* collections were completely correct, and that they themselves had been in error. Also, we showed almost ten errors they had made in their five pages of report. Then, while awaiting severe, threatening reproaches in return for the Fruits of Belief and Collections of Defense Speeches Collections, which we had sent to seven government offices, and for the entire *Risale-i Nur*, which had been sent to the Ministry of Justice, and in particular the strong criticisms that had been laid against certain important persons in confidential treatises, they responded extremely leniently. Even like the reassuring letter that had been sent to us by the Prime Minister, they were conciliatory, far from attacking us. All these proved decisively that, as a miracle of Divine Grace, the truths of the *Risale-i Nur* had caused them to study its treatises like a guide, and made those broad circles into a sort of study circle, securing the belief of numerous hesitating or bewildered people, causing us spiritual joy and profit a hundred times greater than our distress.

Then our secret enemies poisoned me and at the same time the late Hafiz Ali, the martyred hero of the *Risale-i Nur*, went to hospital and from there traveled to the Intermediate Realm of the grave in my place; we wept in despair. Before this disaster, I had repeatedly exclaimed on the mountain at Kastamonu, "My brothers, don't give meat to the horse or grass to the lion!" That is, "Don't give all the treatises to everyone, lest they misunderstand them and use them to attack us." At the time when I had so exclaimed, as if he had heard via his spiritual telephone from a distance of seven days' march, Hafiz Ali, may God have mercy on him, wrote to me, "Indeed, my teacher, it is a wonder of the *Risale-i Nur* that it does not give meat to horses or grass to lions. Rather, it gives horses grass and lions meat so that it gave that lion-like *hoja* the treatise on Sincerity." I received his letter seven days later. We made the calculations, and discovered that at the very moment I was shouting out those words on the mountain, he was writing them in his letter.

Thus, just at the time when we were feeling depressed by the death of that hero of the *Risale-i Nur* and the intrigues that our hypocritical enemies undertook against us so that we would be suspected and punished, and when we were worried that I would be taken to hospital on official orders as I was ill from the poison, Divine Grace suddenly came to our aid. Through the sincere prayers of my blessed brothers, the risk of my death from the poison disappeared. According to powerful signs, Hafiz Ali, that blessed martyr, was occupied in his grave with the *Risale-i Nur*, and answered with the *Risale-i Nur* to the questioning angels; and the Denizli hero, Hasan Feyzi, may God have mercy on him, who would serve in his place and work according to his system, and his friends, were serving the *Risale-i Nur* effectively. Since the other prisoners were being reformed by the *Risale-i Nur*, even our enemies supported our being released from prison. Resembling the Companions of the Cave,[24] the *Risale-i Nur* students turned

---

[24] The Companions of the Cave were seven youths who proclaimed their faith in God's Unity in the presence of the polytheist king of the country, and therefore had to shelter in a cave. As a Divine miracle, they slept in the cave for three hundred years, and were awakened to find that their faith had become the official religion of their nation. Having witnessed this, they died and were buried in the cave. See, the Qur'an, Al-Kahf, 18:9-26. They are

that place of ordeal into a cave of the ascetics of former times, and endeavored to write and publish the parts of the *Risale-i Nur* with contented hearts. All of these proved that Divine Grace had come to our aid.

It also occurred to my heart that since leading scholars of the Law such as Imam A'zam Abu Hanifa[25] had suffered imprisonment; since a supreme defender of Islam like Imam Ahmad ibn Hanbal[26] had been severely tormented in prison for the sake of a single issue related to the Qur'an, and had borne it in perfect patience, not remaining silent about the matter in question; and since numerous religious leaders and scholars had offered thanks in complete patience, without being shaken, although they had been subjected to torments far greater than ours, then certainly we were obliged to offer endless thanks for the few troubles we had to suffer in return for the great reward that we gained from the many truths of the Qur'an. Let me describe briefly a manifestation of Divine Grace amidst humankind's wrongful tyranny:

When I was twenty years old I used to repeatedly say, "Like the recluses who withdrew into caves in former times, towards the end of my life I will retreat from social life into a cave or onto a mountain." Also, when I was a prisoner of war in the northeast of

---

known as, the Seven Sleepers, in the West. (Tr.)

[25] Imam A'zam Abu Hanifa, Nu'man ibn Thabit (d. 768): Founded the Hanafi School of Law and one of the greatest Muslim scholars of jurisprudence and deducer of new laws from the Qur'an and Sunnah. He was also well-versed in theology. (Tr.)

[26] Imam Ahmad ibn Hanbal (d., 855): The founder of one of the four Sunni schools of law in Islam. He valiantly suffered persecution for the sake of his religious conviction. His *Musnad* is famous, containing about 40,000 Traditions that he collected. (Tr.)

Russia during the World War I, I decided that I would spend the remaining part of my life in caves. I would withdraw from political and social life. I had had enough of them. Now I see that, in a way far better than my decision and wish, out of compassion for my old age, the Grace of the Lord and the justice of Divine Destiny changed those caves, which I had thought of withdrawing into, into prisons, retreats, and places of ordeal in loneliness and solitary confinement. It had given me Schools of Joseph that are far superior to the mountain caves of ascetics and recluses, and places of solitary confinement so that I might not waste my time. It had both granted me the benefits of the Hereafter that are expected of retreat in caves, and enabled me to carry out a sacred service to the truths of belief and the Qur'an, which is a kind of *jihad*. I had even thought of feigning guilt of some offense and remaining in prison following the acquittal of my friends, with bachelors like Husrev and Feyzi. On some pretext I would have remained in the cell for solitary confinement in order not to meet with people or not to waste my time on useless conversation or egotistical affectation. But Divine Destiny sent us to another place of ordeal. In accordance with the Divine rules, "That which God chooses is what is good," and

"It may well be that you dislike a thing but it is good for you."

—Al-Baqarah, 2: 216

out of compassion for my old age and so that we should work harder in the service of belief, we were charged with duties beyond our will and power in this third School of Joseph.

There are instances of wisdom and three important benefits for the service of the *Risale-i Nur* in the Divine Grace compassionately turning the caves I had thought to withdraw into during my youth, when I had no powerful, secret enemies, into the solitary confinement cells of prison for my old age:

First instance of wisdom and benefit: At this time the *Risale-i Nur* students can gather only in the School of Joseph without harm. Their coming together outside would have both been expensive and caused suspicion. In such a situation it might even have happened that some of those who came to visit me would have spent forty or fifty *liras* but would have had to return after only seeing me for twenty minutes or not seeing me at all. Therefore, I would have willingly chosen the hardship of prison in order to be closer to some of my brothers. This means that prison is a favor and mercy for us.

Second instance of wisdom and benefit: The service to belief at this time through the *Risale-i Nur* is possible through publicizing it everywhere and drawing the attention of those who are in need of it. Thus, our imprisonment draws attention to the *Risale-i Nur* and contributes to its being known. Those who are most stubborn and in most need can find it and preserve their belief; their stubbornness is defeated and they are saved from the danger of going to the other world without belief, and thus the *Risale-i Nur*'s circle of study is widened.

Third instance of wisdom and benefit: The *Risale-i Nur* students who are imprisoned learn from one another's conduct, character, sincerity, and self sacrifice, and they no longer seek worldly benefits in their service through the *Risale-i Nur*. Indeed, since in the School of Joseph they have observed with their own eyes ten or even a hundred spiritual benefits and good results for every hardship and trouble they suffer, through the good results and extensive sincere service to belief, they are able to attain pure sincerity, no longer lowering themselves by seeking lesser, personal benefits.

There is, however, a sorrowful but agreeable point concerning these places of ordeal that concerns me alone. It is as follows:

I have observed the same situation here that I saw in the old *medreses* in my hometown during my youth. For traditionally in the Eastern Provinces, a portion of the needs of the *medrese* students were met from outside the *medrese*. In some *medreses*, their meals were prepared in the *medrese* itself. And there are several other ways in which the *medreses* resembled this place of ordeal. As I watch the prison with a feeling of pleasurable regret and longing, I travel in my imagination to those former sweet times of youth, and forget the difficulties of old age.